"*The Finish Line* is an exceptional depiction of what means to identify a goal, persevere through hardships, and discipline yourself all the way to the Promised Land. Alex Montoya embodies a remarkable spirit of resilience and determination. Along an unbelievable road, Alex has discovered life's greatest lessons—that excellence is not a goal, it's a journey. *The Finish Line* has information that everyone certainly needs to become champions in the game of life."

—Bill Walton,
Basketball Hall of Famer

"Alex Montoya will make you laugh. Heck, sometimes he'll even make you cry. But above all else he'll inspire you to look deep inside yourself and have the faith to overcome whatever obstacles stand between you and your Finish Line."

—Mario Fraioli,
Senior Producer, Competitor.com

"For most people in Alex Montoya's position, *The Finish Line* would have been when he successfully navigated his way through being born with three missing limbs and into America—the land of opportunity. Instead, it was just the starting line. Alex's *Finish Line* is not even in sight as he continues to push past boundaries and overcome adversity. If you are not inspired by this modern-day hero, you might need to check with a physician."

—Dane Rauschenberg,
Extreme Athlete, Speaker,
Author of *See Dane Run*

The Finish Line

The Finish Line

ALEX MONTOYA

TATE PUBLISHING
AND ENTERPRISES, LLC

Published by Tate Publishing & Enterprises, LLC
127 E. Trade Center Terrace | Mustang, Oklahoma 73064 USA
1.888.361.9473 | www.tatepublishing.com

Tate Publishing is committed to excellence in the publishing industry. The company reflects the philosophy established by the founders, based on Psalm 68:11,
"The Lord gave the word and great was the company of those who published it."

Book design copyright © 2012 by Tate Publishing, LLC. All rights reserved.
Cover design by Joel Uber
Interior design by Caypeeline Casas

Published in the United States of America

ISBN: 978-1-62295-068-3
1. Biography & Autobiography / Sports
2. Sports & Recreation / Running & Jogging
12.10.25

TABLE OF CONTENTS

FOREWORD

Alex Montoya and I have been on a journey together since 2004. Alex tells of our meeting in his first book, *Swinging for the Fences*, although my take may be a bit different. I was an adult facilitator at a youth leadership camp where we listened to a number of speakers. All were good, but then there was Alex.

He strolled up the middle aisle fist bumping with his prosthetic hooks that serve as hands. He had a pronounced limp that I later learned was from his prosthetic leg. I had been around plenty of people with disabilities before, but none who had been born missing both arms and a leg. This young man moved my heart and soul. He does to this day and always will.

So fast forward a bit to the first time I traveled with Alex. We were heading to Las Vegas where Alex was the keynote speaker at the annual Aflac regional meeting. I picked Alex up at his house and as he got seated I said, "Alex, my man, treat me like I am five and just tell me what you do and do not need help with." Alex's reply was: "No problem—you can start with fastening my seat belt and by the way, you have never traveled until you see me go through security."

Boy was he right! He also told me that people were going to stare and to not let it bother me—they did and it did.

I watched Alex being patted down, waved over with handheld metal detectors again and again, a supervisor being called in. To me it looked humiliating. Then I looked closer. Alex was smiling the entire time and chatting up the oh-so-friendly TSA agents— just another day for him.

As you read this book you will get a real feeling for Alex. For his sense of humor, his drive, his passion, and his faith. But, I want you to get something else. I want you to imagine taking off your arms and a leg at night and putting them on in the morning. I want you to think about the simple things you do— tying your shoes, unwrapping a piece of candy, cutting up a nice steak— and how it would be if your hands were prosthetic hooks.

Now, imagine that when you are around Alex, when you get to know him, that you no longer see the prosthetics. You just see an amazing and inspiring man who can do anything to which he sets his mind. And, he wants you to know that YOU can too. So, when Alex told me he was going to run a marathon, my response was not one of disbelief or doubt. I believe I said something like, "That's great. Which one and when?"

I was humbled to be asked to write this foreword. Alex is a bright spot in my life, and I know he will be one in yours as well.

By the way, Alex does love a good steak, craves sweets, will dance until the sun comes up, is a sports maniac, a believer, an inspiration, and my friend.

—Jim Ponder

ACKNOWLEDGMENTS

Every Sunday, as often as I can, I have a personal tradition. I'll equip myself with music, mesh shorts, and all my thoughts and concerns, and take a long stroll around my neighborhood. Running takes too much of a toll on my back and left leg at this stage of my life, so in the past few years, I have gone from running to walking. I think it's better this way anyway. I can still walk at a brisk pace and heighten my cardiovascular exercise. And I can hone in on my thoughts better.

I've done this for many years, starting when I lived in a metropolis part of San Diego to my neighborhood of the past decade, which is more residential and surrounded by steep, concrete hills, sweeping canyons, and a winding sidewalk that stretches for a good two miles. The landscape is diverse enough yet still familiar, where one can get lost in the pulsating music and end-of-the-week thoughts.

In all my years of taking these sojourns, usually lasting one to two hours as the sun sets, I think of everything and nothing at once. I can't tell you of any imminent decisions I've ever made on these walks.

Except one.

In the early spring of 2010, I had a desire to write a follow-up book to my 2008 authorial debut, *Swinging for the Fences*. Knowing that the creative and editing process often takes a year or more—much longer than most people seem to think—I wanted to make sure I had a story or topic that would hold my interest in writing it and the reader's interest in consuming it. A few weeks prior, I had committed to paper a budding idea—a letter with life advice penned to my nephew Noah. It seemed a good way to dispense ideas that then-two-year old Noah could enjoy in later years. But after writing a couple draft chapters, I was suddenly stuck.

Looking at my watch, the thought struck me that I only had an hour to go to complete my goal of three miles walked. I had set this benchmark as early training for the upcoming San Diego Rock 'n' Roll Marathon.

Instantly, it hit me! A letter to Noah or other youth might someday happen. But this is what I was experiencing right *now*! I was a man with three prosthetics, who had never participated in an endurance race, walking on a relay team with three women who were able-bodied but also devoid of race experience. This was a very difficult challenge.

So I decided to write about it. The result, two years later, is this book.

In between that lightning flash of an idea to the pages cradled in your hands was the involvement and assistance of many people. In giving thanks, if I forget anyone, please charge it to my head and not my heart.

My first thanks goes to Almighty God, for blessing me with the ability and inspiration to write. I hope this book serves as a reminder of what can be achieved through faith and determination, because as Luke 1:37 says, "All things are possible." For their constant encouragement and support, I thank my two mothers, Ines and Lucia, and their families in Colombia and the United States. I also thank my angel in heaven, Elizabeth.

I am incredibly fortunate to work for the San Diego Padres Baseball Club. In addition to supporting my responsibilities as Manager of Latino Affairs, my writing and public speaking endeavors are graciously encouraged by President Tom Garfinkel and Senior Vice-President of Public Affairs, Sarah Farnsworth. In Vice-President of Community Relations Sue Botos, I have a boss of remarkable depth, humor, and friendship. The entire staff of the Padres is a family for which I am most grateful.

A world of thanks to Dr. Richard Tate, Lindsey Marcus, and everyone at Tate Publishing in Mustang, Oklahoma, for publishing this prose. It has been an honor publishing both of my books with you. Thank you to Jim Ponder, Kelly

Ponder, and Turnkey Strategic Relations in Escondido, CA, for working hard to secure the publishing contract – but more so for their lifelong friendship. Once Tate and Turnkey negotiated a contract, Lidia Martinez and Southwest Airlines came through in a major way to ensure our project was off to a good start. Lidia donated two Southwest Airlines tickets as a raffle prize for a pre-sale that we held, and I am extremely thankful to those who purchased entries.

My gratitude to Bill Walton, Dave Dravecky, Dane Rauschenberg, and Mario Fraioli for their extremely kind-hearted testimonials. A special word of thanks to Fraioli's employer, Competitor Group International (CGI), for supporting this book and also for including the relay as an option for their San Diego marathon. It allowed people like me, who had never previously undertaken such an endeavor, to try it. For that I am eternally grateful. It occurs to me that in 1990, Congress passed the Americans with Disabilities Act. Some twenty-two years later, groups like CGI are ensuring the civil rights law is bolstered with real-life opportunity.

I also received constant love and encouragement from both staff and alumni connected to the University of Notre Dame—Go Irish!—and the University of San Francisco. I am proud to be a graduate of both institutions.

Frankly, I am proud to have attempted this race and written this book. Both took consistent and unyielding faith, discipline, and determination. The pennant race between the Padres and Giants serves as a fitting backdrop because the baseball season is like a marathon and a marathon—as you will see, is a lot like life.

It is not easy wearing three prosthetics day after day—and certainly not easy walking several miles or writing several chapters with them. But it is not impossible. And that's what I want you to get out of reading this. Obstacles and challenges are real but with faith, determination, and teamwork...all things are possible.

—Alex Montoya

KEEP SWINGING

On October 7, 2008, *Swinging for the Fences: Choosing to Live an Extraordinary Life*, my personal story of overcoming challenges as a triple amputee from birth and immigrating from Colombia to the United States to achieve my dreams, was released nationally and my life was changed forever. I didn't become wealthy or famous. I didn't quit my job at the San Diego Padres. Heck, Oprah still didn't invite me onto her show or book club.

But for me, it was the culmination of a lifelong goal and dream—publishing a book. Subsequently, the book signings, speaking engagements, and one-on-one interactions with people who read it impacted me more than I could have ever imagined. Those encounters were what really touched and changed me.

I didn't do a book tour, per se, but was invited to a few different cities to do a signing or speak, or both. When my undergraduate alma mater, Notre Dame, played at the

University of Washington in football, I flew to blustery Seattle in late October and spoke at the Fighting Irish pep rally the night before the game at a downtown hotel. I probably enjoyed the Irish blowout win a little bit less than I did hearing the roar of the one thousand fans in the ballroom when I said, "Notre Dame was expensive…soooo expensive…it cost me an arm and a leg."

Sorry. It's my signature line.

A shorter trip was made from my hometown, beautiful San Diego, to Long Beach. There I met a small business owner who said he happened to stumble upon the flyer advertising my Saturday afternoon talk at a local café. He was down on himself because his small business was not doing well. He was ready to give it up, in fact. By the end of my talk, he had decided to not sell his struggling business and indeed *keep swinging*. I was truly amazed that my book could have this type of impact. People had told me they were motivated to overcome their challenges after reading how I overcame mine. That had always elicited a feeling of pride within me. But to meet a gentleman who had not read the book yet, but was about to do so after hearing my presentation and to see that he was inspired to not give up on his business – his personal dream – left me feeling astounded and humbled.

One weekend found me in Laughlin, Nevada, where a lady had a brother who was a firefighter and just lost his arm. She didn't know what to tell him. Now she knew she could provide him some consolation and hope.

I say all this not to impress you, but to impress *upon* you that dreams come true. That when you achieve a goal, you're not only doing something for yourself but giving hope and motivation to others.

Whether it was at a bookstore in the South Bay part of San Diego, to the high school girls' field hockey team taught by a friend of mine, to various luncheons or dinners, I met incredible people overcoming incredible adversities.

I got to return to Notre Dame and do a signing at the palatial bookstore there, which was colossally gratifying because many old college friends and my mentor, Bob Mundy, were in attendance.

I've spoken before hundreds at Rotary Club breakfasts and to an audience of five at a Kiwanis Club meeting. Audience numbers don't matter to me. I love talking and at every single speaking engagement or book signing, I am just amazed people have an interest in what I have to say.

People told me in those first few months after *Swinging* was released that it helped them overcome fears, counsel drug-addicted siblings, have a better attitude toward their disabilities, and push them toward their true passions in life. As a writer, I already felt proud to have published a book. But to hear that it was impacting people's life decisions made me even more proud and gratified. It also made me feel that all the adversity I faced was more than worth it because others were relating their challenges to mine and overcoming them. This was not a pride borne out of vanity but out of amazement.

My head wouldn't have been able to fit through the door had I not remembered that all of this was a blessing from God. Not to mention the years of struggle just to get that book published.

For over a year I felt absolutely thrilled any time a copy of the book found its way into my mailbox and got a real kick out of signing and returning it to addresses located from California to Kentucky. One elementary school in New Jersey asked for a copy to be dedicated to its campus library. Even one of *Swinging's* protagonists, University of Notre Dame President Emeritus, Edward "Monk" Malloy, included it in his literature class curriculum, which by itself blew me away and then *truly* stunned me when he had a student videotape the class discussion. It was surreal, yet humbling.

By the time 2009 had ended, completing a full year of speaking engagements and media interviews promoting the book, I felt satisfied. As I told the hundreds of families at the National Catholic Conference at the Anaheim Convention Center, or the networking luncheons with twenty people in attendance, you have to pursue your greatest dream and swing for the fences instead of settling for safer, less desirable goals.

Indeed, I had achieved my mission of adding *author* to my list of life milestones: college graduate, Master's degree recipient, baseball executive. Places I never envisioned would be interested in my story certainly proved otherwise and I even did a telephone interview with a Pennsylvania radio station and a nationally syndicated (*Sí TV*) show on cable.

It blew my mind and was a perpetual thrill ride.

So 2010 crept into my life and with it came a question. It was like a strong wind. I didn't know where it started but I could certainly feel it: *What dream do I chase now?*

Mind you, it wasn't like I was done promoting the book or that my job handling the Latino community marketing and outreach for the Padres was minimal. Both were as busy as ever. My job entails connecting the Padres to the Latino community via our charitable outreach, community programs, and Spanish-language website (*www.padresbeisbol.com*) and Facebook page. That's a full load during the day and includes attending evening community functions as well.

But I knew I wanted—and needed—a brand new challenge.

As the New Year unfolded, still fresh in its dew, a co-worker of mine at the Padres, Steve Carter, extended an invitation to attend an information session one frosty January evening. He had been very active with an organization called *Team in Training* and had raised funds through them for three marathons. The fundraising was all for the Leukemia and Lymphoma Society (LLS).

Along with several other colleagues I sat and listened to three highly exuberant individuals describe how much they enjoyed running marathons and raising money for LLS. Fairly quickly, I knew the fundraising aspect wasn't something I wanted to try, at least not in this year, with a heavy workload in front of me. Besides, I knew I could help their great cause by contributing to my friends' fundraising.

But this marathon idea sounded intriguing. At once it seemed grueling, daunting, inspiring, and wonderful. My curiosity was piqued.

The San Diego Rock 'n' Roll Marathon would be held on June 6, 2010 and, as it had since its inception and now was re-created in several other cities, would be a 26.2-mile course spanning the city.

The first "RnR", which as you can imagine, provides anything but rest and relaxation, was in 1998. That year holds a special place in my heart because it was when the Padres overcame heavy odds to reach the World Series for only the second time in club history.

I actually attended the '98 RnR post-race concert because it was held in Balboa Stadium, the stadium of my alma mater, San Diego High School, so I knew where to sneak in. That concert featured 1980s rock paragons Pat Benatar and Huey Lewis, the latter whom I saw backstage among the post-show food spread. Yes, I snuck backstage and of course found the buffet table. Huey Lewis pointed at my two prosthetic hooks. Holding a carne asada taco, he said, "You have two of those."

Very astute, Huey. *The Heart of Rock 'n' Roll is Still Beatin'*.

Some twelve years later, listening to these speakers and growing increasingly excited about the idea, I wondered what ol' venerable rock legend Huey would think. I did, still, after all, "have two of those" prosthetic arms and hooks. I still had a prosthetic leg on my right side. Although I had played intramural soccer at Notre Dame, and jogged or walked on my own just as exercise and a stress-reliever, I'd never come close to doing a marathon.

As I was preparing to leave and my equally excited co-workers were signing up then and there, my buddy Jacob Dubois grabbed me by the "SD" label on the chest of my San Diego Padres jacket. "You know you're doing this, right?" he nodded. "Even if you don't do a full, the half marathon is thirteen miles. You can do it."

It reminded me of the life-influencing day when my childhood friend Margarita Farrales (now Fox) forced me onto the monkey bars at Charles Lindbergh Elementary. She knew I'd always wanted to try it and would never know if I could or could not unless I attempted it.

"Try climbing the monkey bars, we'll all be here to help you," Margarita said in that Benatar/Lewis era. "You can do it."

That day I climbed and, although it may sound like a small feat for those who can take things like that for granted, it showed me I can scale new heights. I can try new goals. I can take chances and dream unlikely dreams.

I had written a book. I had attained my desired profession. I had lived out several dreams.

Now I wanted to try a marathon.

Was I crazy?

THIS IS MADNESS

A few short months after *Swinging for the Fences* was released, I was adjusting to balancing various speaking requests while making sure I was properly handling my duties at the San Diego Padres. The ball club was tremendously supportive and fortunately, most book signings and such were on weekends and evenings. Plus, it was the 2008 off-season, so there weren't any games at those times anyway.

The funny thing about life, though, is the only constant is change. Nothing changed in terms of their support of my writing but a major change with the club occurred within the first day of 2009.

John Moores, who had owned the Padres since December 1994, had announced a few months earlier he was selling the team. The first Sunday of the New Year I was at the Colts-Chargers playoff game in San Diego when news broke that a new owner would be sought. Like with any corporate change, one knew there would be changes but no one could foretell, of course, exactly how and when.

I learned some invaluable lessons in this time period that I think could be of benefit to others.

The greatest fear swirled around would there be any staff changes. I would be dishonest if I said that question hadn't crossed my mind, especially relative to *my* job. But I knew there was plenty to do in marketing and outreaching to the San Diego-Tijuana Latino community and that kept me occupied. Still, you can't help but notice when people have anxiety or speculate on potential changes.

It reminded me a bit of a situation I was in a decade earlier, at the San Diego County Hispanic Chamber of Commerce. Knowing that my long-term goal was to work for the Padres, I took a part-time job as an usher on their game day staff. But I needed something with more hours and benefits to augment that job.

Having been an active member and volunteer with the Hispanic Chamber, I didn't hesitate when they offered a membership sales position. My friends, including some I knew on the Chamber staff, were puzzled, however. Why would I take a position that was actually a *temporary* job? The offer, in fact, was that I would work from August 1999 until October '99 for a salary, plus sales commission, and then the Chamber would either hire me and provide benefits or, simply, cut me loose.

"Why take such a risky position?" one friend asked me.

"Because," I told her, I wasn't focusing solely on the risks. All I needed to focus on was doing well from August through October. Sure enough, I did well enough that cutting me loose wasn't seriously considered. But they didn't hire me either. I was offered the chance to extend that temporary contract through December.

I jumped at it.

"Why would you prolong such a risk?" someone inquired.

Because what I saw was not the risk, but the opportunity. Just like I don't focus on my disabilities but rather on the incredible opportunities for fun and success found in this greatest of countries, I focused on the good. The Hispanic Chamber was a rising business networking organization that had just moved to a larger office in a growing part of the city, downtown, in a time when San Diego and Hispanic business in general was starting to boom.

I never said securing new and renewed members would be easy but the potential was there for great success. Plus I knew the organization like I knew the Padres roster, and more importantly, I knew myself. I knew I had the drive and work ethic and if I focused on that, good things would happen. I didn't focus on impressing my Chamber bosses. I just focused on doing a great job, period. So great that retaining me would be a no-brainer and if they didn't hire me, someone else would.

I didn't focus on the problem or challenge but purely on the solution. The rest would take care of itself. I adopted a philosophy of "Personal Attention" and each one of our five hundred members received a letter and/or phone call from me when they joined or renewed. It took some late hours and I probably blew through our mailing budget, but the members appreciated it. Eventually five hundred members grew to over nine hundred.

January 2000 came and with the new millenium, a new job offer by the Chamber. They retained me and I stayed with the Hispanic Chamber, with the Padres as my evening and weekend job, for seven more years. I love that because seven is my favorite number.

Flash forward to 2009 and the uncertainty with the Padres ownership change. How would I overcome the fear of these changes and potentially the difficulty in adapting to whatever was headed our way?

Again, what I focused upon was doing my job well. Whether it was coordinating Hispanic-themed events like Fiesta con los Padres, which included a special postgame concert, or advising the club on charitable requests from Hispanic-focused organizations, I focused on those. That's all I could control.

Whoever was going to run the team, what good would it do if I had a negative reputation within the community? Or what if my bosses stayed intact but couldn't look our new supervisors squarely in the eye to tell them I should be retained?

So really, I looked at it as an opportunity. As with any ownership or management change, which eventually begets change at the staff level, we were all being evaluated. That drove me to work harder, put in longer hours, and be more aggressive about spreading the Gospel of Padres Baseball.

I also took on new responsibilities, like seeking out and coordinating Padres marketing booths at grassroots community events. Whenever I attended these street fairs or carnivals, I noticed the longest lines were for booths that had prize wheels. People spun them and after the clack-clack-clack came applause and the feeling that something terrific, even if it was a small promotional item like a keychain, had been won. Thus, we ordered one and marketing the crack of the bat became synonymous with clack-clack-clack. Like my Chamber mentality, I wanted it to be a no-brainer. Either the Padres would keep me or someone else would. Eventually there were indeed changes and between our management change, and a struggling economy, we endured staff layoffs.

I was, thanks be to God, retained when a new management team came in. But that didn't mean change didn't affect me. In addition to seeing friends and co-workers let go, the department I was in was restructured.

That meant a change in job responsibilities and a new locale as we were shifted to another floor. A prospective new team owner and management meant we had to learn a new system, a new paradigm, and, as fate would have it, market a new team to the public because the playing roster was getting an overhaul and new blood was putting on gloves and picking up bats.

2009 was a new era.

It wasn't easy on or off the field. With so many young players, coupled with injuries to veterans, the '09 Padres struggled early. Meanwhile, we were given a mandate to promote the "SD" brand as heavily as possible, from wearing it on our attire to blanketing the city with that logo. We took on new events, an aggressive approach, and pushed harder.

It was certainly a time of adjustment. In time, though, we adapted and even new staff members felt like part of the family within a short period. We recognized that we were all in this together and change could be exciting and invigorating. We were a part of something new. The players helped add to the enthusiasm when they went through a metamorphosis as well. As they gained experience and confidence, they closed July on a winning streak.

Then August was filled with walk-off homers and renewed enthusiasm. Finally, in the final month of the season, September, the Padres started impacting other teams' playoff chances by continually winning. By the time the season closed and autumn descended on San Diego, our Friars compiled a 37-25 mark over the final 62 games—fourth-best in the entire league.

It made for a fall of budding optimism and renewed fire.

That dovetailed into the beginning of 2010 when my colleagues and I, perhaps sensing greatness on the horizon, sought new challenges and adventures.

The more I reflected on what I'd heard on that clear, cold January evening from the Team in Training representatives, the more I felt motivated. My heart was stirred. I wanted to do a marathon. But here's the thing with dreams or ambitious goals: you always need a Plan B.

I knew my first step was to inform my prosthetist. Jonathan Skerritt and Hangar Prosthetics, located in the uptown district of Hillcrest in San Diego, had created and repaired my prosthetic limbs since early in my Chamber days. Some people know you like the back of their hand. Well, Jonathan knew me like the back of my hooks because he made them.

I made an appointment and told him self-assuredly I was entering a marathon. His reaction surprised me. Did he laugh or reject the idea? No, and that was the surprise because it was such a wild idea I thought he might.

"Alex, my man," Jonathan said, placing his large hand calloused by many prosthetic limb repairs, "you can do anything you want. Hangar will support you. But how 'bout you talk to your physician first and make sure your body can sustain this?"

I nodded.

"Oh," Jonathan added, "and what about something besides the full marathon? Is there a half or a relay team?"

Indeed there was and judging by his lithe, slender frame, I should've figured my prosthetist was probably a runner himself and an expert in that sport.

For the first time since its inception, the Rock 'n' Roll San Diego was adding a thirteen-mile half-marathon, plus allowing relay teams of four to divide up the entire 26.2 miles.

My doctor, the caring and often nervous (because he cared about his patients so much), Dr. Ho liked this Plan B very much. Fearing strain not only on my limbs but also pulmonary and cardiovascular systems, he ruled out a full marathon. A half marathon? Possible, he told me. A relay team? Ideal.

The next thing you need besides a Plan B is someone with whom you can share that dream; not just a supporter but someone equally invested.

I knew *Swinging for the Fences* would become a reality when Jim Ponder approached me at a Rotary camp for kids in Idyllwild, CA in 2005 and said, "I believe in your vision. Let's get your book written."

I knew participating in a marathon would be a reality when I shared this idea with a few friends. No one scoffed. The majority said, "Right on!" A couple said, "Wow," and just looked incredulous. But Karen Madden, my co-worker who since 2002 had coordinated national anthems, ballpark entertainers, special events, and a slew of other

Entertainment responsibilities at beautiful Petco Park, didn't bat an eye.

"I'll do it."

"What?" I asked her.

"I'll do a marathon with you. Why not? Sounds like fun." I was amazed she would agree so readily and felt really quite touched. Participating in a marathon *couldn't* be as easy or carefree as Karen was making it out to be. I sensed she was making it that way to show support to me.

Karen Madden, or K-Mad as she's affectionately known at 100 Park Boulevard, had never run a marathon. She had always been an avid cheerleader and volleyball player growing up in Nebraska but, as she puts it, "I hate running."

But it sounded fun to her and she wanted me to be able to try it. We still needed two more teammates but I knew having K-Mad on board would attract others.

Jonathan approved. Dr. Ho approved. I looked at Karen one stormy day in late January as we discussed training schedules.

"This is going to take serious planning," she said. "We're going to have to find out how long each leg of the course is and find two more people willing to do that instance. It's almost February, which means baseball season is two months away and the marathon is only *four* months away. We have to start training right away."

"I know," I replied with concern in my voice, "and frankly I haven't walked or jogged more than two miles in several months."

Just as quickly, Karen Madden's tone turned from stern to upbeat, "It'll be hard but it'll be fun. It's like what you always say when the Padres are in a close match, 'We can win this game.'"

The enormity of the task ahead still overwhelmed me, though.

Chuckling, I said, "A gimp and a non-runner and who knows who else…doing a marathon. We call you K-Mad. In this case, it's also really appropriate. Because this is madness."

MARATHON MAN

Often a goal or dream is met not with resistance, but skepticism. You can't really blame people for being skeptical; you just have to show them why you are a believer. Hopefully they'll become believers too.

Karen Madden—from whom Team MADness derived its name—and I found ourselves leaning upon two friends named Colleen in late winter. Colleen McDonald, a graduate school classmate of mine who worked for Competitor Group, who put on all the Rock 'n' Roll Marathons nationally, supplied us with key information: the 26.2-mile course would be divided into four legs for relay teams, meaning each relay runner would be enduring between five to eight miles average.

"I think it's awesome you're trying this but it won't be easy," she said, invoking her three years of working on marathons across the country. "But with the last leg being the shortest and the flattest ground, across Fiesta Island, I think that's your best bet."

Fiesta Island is a beachfront piece of land connecting the city to Mission Bay, and I had never been there, let alone walked across it for five miles, so I was hopeful but skeptical myself.

Downright doubtful was our other Colleen, a co-worker with the last name McEniry, who K-Mad and I asked to join our relay team. She was an excellent softball player and was known to be a scrappy athlete and we liked that kind of attitude. Her doubtfulness, though, wasn't directed toward us.

"Me, run a marathon?" McEniry pointed a finger inwards and jutted her head outwards.

"Sure, why not?" Karen responded.

"Because I haven't run in months," said McEniry, responding to what was supposed to be a rhetorical question. "I play softball. I run from first to third and second to home. I don't run *marathons*."

Her uttering of the word "marathon" wasn't said with contempt, but rather with incredulousness. Still, we asked Colleen to think it over and hoped that it would be appealing to her that a number of her close friends—who had motivated me—were already signed up to do the full or half-marathon individually.

"Look," said the Irish girl who stood about five-four and loved to gesticulate while talking, "Opening Day is only a few weeks away and I've got plenty of work to do. Plus I've got my second job, and Mike and I just moved into a new apartment, and the neighborhood of our new apartment isn't ideal for evening running, which is the only time I could do that."

By now McEniry was counting these reasons with her fingers, each point leading her to slap a finger on her left arm with a finger from her right.

She was right, too. Our Padres home opener was rapidly approaching, April 12 looming large in every ball club employee's conscience. Actually, to most sports fans, because February was barely blending into March, there was more talk about college and pro basketball than baseball. But when you work in Major League Baseball, as soon as New Year's Day passes, it's baseball pre-season, with deadlines and an increased workload making Opening Day seem like mere hours away.

Also accurate were Colleen's assertions that she and her boyfriend had a new pad and that between her evening job and urban neighborhood, jogging past sunset was not a great idea.

"But if you guys really think you can do this," she sighed, "and if you think I can contribute…(another sigh)…yeah, I'll do it."

K-Mad and I whooped and then spontaneously celebrated, her fist bumping my hook while we each made the sound of exploding fireworks.

It looked like smooth sailing from that point forward.

We had three members of our requisite four man—make that four-person team. When word spread about our relay team, another co-worker, Maribel Castro in Ticket Services, asked if she could join us.

"Heck yeah!" I affirmed, knowing K-Mad wouldn't oppose and would, in fact, welcome Maribel.

As early spring entered like a fresh morning breeze, I charted out a course of preparation. Our Director of Security, Ken Kawachi, who seemingly knew everything about beautiful Petco Park, told me that the perimeter outside the ballpark was a total of .75. So if I exited the front lobby doors on 100 Park Boulevard, walked one long block, and then made a series of left turns at the end of each subsequent block—like a NASCAR driver, except with purpose—and then wound up back at the lobby, I would have walked three-quarters of a mile.

Knowing that I needed to walk five on June 6, I planned on tackling that goal, .75 miles at a time.

After work each night, I donned a blue Padres long-sleeve cotton shirt and prepared to start my training. Because I have trouble manipulating an iPod with my hooks, I asked K-Mad to help place a pair of Walkman earphones on my head.

"A Walkman?" she cringed. "What is this, 1996?"

I ignored her barbs about my antiquated music device, just as I did when she chided me for spending up to fifteen minutes stretching. "Hey, I don't want to tighten up, what can I say? I'm a stretcher," I said to her while loosening up my foot, back, neck, and hips.

Only .75 miles? This would be easy! I could knock that out in a half-hour, if not less, and by the end of two hours, I will have walked five or six miles. Plus it was barely March, so by April I would be at seven miles and by June, I'd ramp up to eight. That'll make five miles on June 6 seem like a stroll.

In college I played on an intramural soccer team and as a young adult I was an avid jogger. Energy has never been a problem, as anyone who's shared a dance floor with me can attest. But jogging can take a toll on one's body, which is why the last couple of years had seen me jog less and walk more. That didn't affect my conditioning as much as the fact that due to working, writing, speaking, and general shenanigans, I hadn't walked for exercise in months.

It showed.

Shooting off like an adrenaline-fueled rocket, which was my first mistake, the end of the first lap saw me slowing down. Mentally I was determined and the beats of Black Eyed Peas and other hip-hop/R&B artists pumping through my headphones still had me hyped. But it was like my Adidas sneakers had sandbags attached.

Sweat was pouring from my temples and breathing became an accelerated pace. My back started stiffening up too, which led me to twist and turn and stretch in order to loosen it. Imagine you're a jogger in downtown San Diego and in front of you is a man with two hooks, a limp (my prosthetic leg was covered by pants because of the early spring cool weather), an ancient Walkman, and he's twisting his torso as he speed-walks.

That wouldn't look strange, would it?

There was never any doubt that I wouldn't complete two hours worth of walking. I had resolve and, although I was nearing a couple hundred pounds, or as my best buds at work would call it "a couple bills", I also wasn't in danger of appearing on *The Biggest Loser*.

What was discouraging was that after two hours, on an ideal, crisp evening, full of adrenaline and nervous energy, I only completed two laps: one and a half (sweaty) miles. That's it.

Although we still needed a fourth person, Karen and Colleen McEniry figured the first three runners would need to finish their leg in an hour or so. That would give me a little extra time and Colleen McDonald reminded us that relay teams needed to be done within seven hours.

But at this rate, one and a half miles in two hours, how the heck was I going to walk five miles?

Equally discouraging were people's thoughts about the Padres. Despite the 37-25 finish the previous season, fans just saw a team that was young, unknown, and with the majors' lowest payroll.

But life is about focusing on what you have and not on what you're missing. Sometimes *you* just need to believe in order for others to believe.

Everyone, and I mean everyone, was picking against the Padres heading into 2010. Fans. Journalists. ESPN. The MLB Network. *USA Today*. Every website in cyberspace. They didn't just pick us not to win the division, they universally said we'd finish last—in the National League West and perhaps all of baseball.

This is how the Padres organization believed and showed others: when they talked about the past, we talked about the future.

We hosted several Open Houses and talked about how the previous season's tough lumps would yield a team of increased maturity and experience. Looking at our playing roster we knew the national media saw only one or two household names, but we knew the lesser-known players were fast, skilled, and aggressive. We knew, too, we were building a solid pitching staff. We also adopted a new policy whereby to demonstrate our pride in beautiful Petco Park, instead of trying to sell people tickets over the phone, we invited them to the ballpark for free tours. We believed in our team and our venue and customers needed to see that.

We knew no one was going to believe in the 2010 Padres. No one except us.

Similarly, when people asked me how my initial marathon workouts had gone, I was honest. I had improved somewhat but was still struggling to do more than two laps in two hours. A third lap to break the two-mile mark was a grueling affair.

Although no one told me flat-out I couldn't do it, many looked resigned, as if they had perhaps expected it. I heard: *it's ok, you tried your best.*

No way! I knew I could do better and I must. In fact, I would text-message my nightly results to Karen, McEniry, and Maribel, and after weeks of "Hang in there" responses but not much progress, K-Mad wrote back exactly what I needed to hear.

She wrote:

We are busting our butts to make this happen. Time to step it up, buddy.

Our team leader was right. The others had generously granted me the opportunity to complete the final leg so the terrain would be flatter and I could experience the thrill of crossing the finish line.

"If we give you, say, between two and two-and-a-half hours, will that be enough time?" K-Mad asked one day at Lolita's Taco Shop across the street from Petco Park.

Taking a half-crunchy, half-soft bite at a marvel of food called the Two-in-One—two rolled tacos inside of a burrito—I nodded.

"That should work," McEniry added, "because if Alex takes two hours, us three have five hours total to complete our portion before he does his. It won't be easy but we'll have to run as fast as we can."

That sparked both a sense of motivation and embarrassment within me. These girls, none of whom had ever done a marathon, were buying into my dream. In order to make that dream a reality they were looking for ways to decrease their time and speed up their pace.

As I pondered this, a text was rattling its way through my vibrating cell phone. It was from Colleen McDonald: *Esquith & Sandoval r in for R 'n' R–Fillmore Frank too!*

I figured out what she meant.

Our buddies from the University of San Francisco Sport Management Master's Program, Josh Esquith and Jonathan Sandoval, along with Jonathan's best friend, Frank Marrufo, from the Ventura County town of Fillmore, had signed up to do the Rock 'n' Roll.

I texted McDonald back with a stream of Padres staff names that had also caught race fever: Nina Tarantino, Katie Leisz, Krystal Di Stefano, and Jacob Dubois.

All were our friends and each name was another example of someone I wanted to see at the finish line. I looked at my Two-in-One and I'd be lying to you if I said I threw it down and vowed off all Mexican food until race day!

No, I simply said to myself: less fast food. More consistent walking just to increase my stamina. Then on the weekends, longer walks for better conditioning, and eventually work on decreasing my time.

It was more a prudent plan, filled less with bravado and more with earnest sensibility. I didn't want to let all my friends down that were doing this race and most important, I didn't want to fail my teammates.

It didn't take long to put the plan into action. Two to three weeknights, Karen helped with my old-school Walkman; I'd listen to hip-hop and old-school R&B; I'd stretch like crazy; and I'd walk several laps in two to three hours. On my way home, in good nights and bad, I'd text my results to K-Mad, McEniry, and Maribel.

This continued for several weeks and I was starting to shed a few "bills" and feel good. I was completing .75 in closer to a half-hour, which meant I was reaching two to four miles if I really pushed it.

Sometimes a dream requires reassessing and adjusting your goals. Sometimes the only way to make believers out of doubters is to keep grinding.

Sometimes a dream also requires the ability to withstand a challenge—including those that figuratively smack you in the face.

The first week of April dawned and Colleen was running in the mornings before her two jobs, and Karen and Maribel would run before or after work. I was walking in the evening and excited about my improved times and the Padres season that was finally upon us.

As for the Padres, any baseball fan with a daily passion and caring for his or her team tends to call their squad the *boys* or *lads*. My boys had just completed a spring training schedule in Peoria, Arizona—where they continued last season's torrid finish with another long win streak—and for the season opener stayed right there in Phoenix to face the Diamondbacks.

Opening Day everywhere, anywhere, is full of optimism, cheer, joy, and hope. I relished how these Padres would prove the naysayers wrong, starting today.

Thud.

That sound you just heard, besides the crack of the bat from Arizona's players, was the sound of hopes falling flat. The lads fell behind right away and we lost. Dan Haren, the Diamondbacks pitching ace, kept them in that hole, looking near-unhittable.

Leaving work that night, I encountered a fan eyeballing the prices listed on a ticket window.

"Hey, hey, it's Opening Day!" I said cheerfully to him as I stretched for a quick workout. "Uh, you looking to buy some tickets when the box office re-opens tomorrow?"

The fan looked at me in disgust, saying with a snarl, "Maybe later this summer. I saw the game on TV today. Same ol' Padres."

Before I could respond, my phone had a familiar hum. It was a text from Maribel, asking me to call her right away. I pride myself on the lost art of memorizing phone numbers so I mentally recalled her number and dialed her up.

"A-Mo, I am so sorry."

"For what?" I asked.

"Well," Maribel sighed, "I just got offered a sales job by the Washington Nationals and I think I'd like to take it."

"Maribel, that's great! This is an opportunity for you to advance your sports career!"

"Aw, thanks, A-Mo…but you know what this means, right?"

Then it hit me like a Dan Haren curveball. We were about to lose our relay teammate.

KEEP IT FRESH

It always amuses me when new trends or words emerge, especially among youths and teens. They are usually old catch phrases, or fashions, that disappear for a few years or even decades and then get re-invented. In my presentations to kids I have seen many old hairstyles, clothing styles, and popular words "created", when in reality they simply came back.

In the early spring of 2010, I was fortunate to speak at a few local graduations for various grade levels, as well as at organizations like Reality Changers, which is an academic and mentoring program for San Diego inner city youth. One of the things I most enjoy is fielding a few questions, which usually range from *What drives you to succeed?* (My faith and the incredible opportunities I've been granted in life) to *Are you married?* (Not yet but I am accepting résumés). Then after the ceremony or program, I like to stick around and talk to whomever wants to chat or ask questions individually and up close.

Starting in the previous fall, I noticed that whenever I showed students how my arms worked, or if they put a finger inside my hook to see that it did not hurt, they would marvel with the usual exclamations: *"Cool! Sweet! Tight!"*

But a new one was being uttered. One I heard, and said, back when I was in junior high and looking for an adjective to describe Tony Gwynn's batting stroke or Michael Jordan's, well, everything:

"Fresh!"

The word even made its way into the adult world when a co-worker like Jake Dubois, Nick Golden, or Mark Matsunaga would get a haircut and extol each other for a "fresh fade". It was an adjective and verb combined.

I knew, then, that I had a word that could get the kids' attention—they're always surprised when adults actually speak their language—as well as describe what my marathon teammates were trying to do.

We were keeping it *Fresh*. It dawned upon me that in life, in order to overcome obstacles and be a champion, one needed to keep it *Fresh*. In other words, to rely upon:

*F*aith
*R*elationships
*E*nergy
*S*taying Connected

*H*itting a Homer (Swinging for the Fences!)

You need faith to keep you going—spiritually and in yourself and your dreams.

You need relationships that are positive and encouraging and, in this world, your chances for success are maximized if you have strong relationships within your field. Sometimes with kids I'll remind them that *R* can also stand for respect—of others, of your dream or profession, and most importantly, yourself.

You need to exert energy toward your dream and you know a path is the right one when you feel energy within yourself.

Staying connected is what you must do on a variety of levels. Each and every day stay connected to your faith, your family, your ideals, and your life dream. Also, just as cables and straps help my arms to stay connected, so must you in a networking sense.

Finally, hit a homer. Don't just think small or take a check swing in life. Go for it all! Swing for the Fences! Try your absolute best and the results will take care of themselves. If your friends doubt your ambitions, are they really your friends?

When it came to Team MADness, Karen and I certainly had Faith—spiritually and in each other. Colleen was getting there, although she was more concerned about lack of training time. We all had *energy* and we were definitely trying to *hit a homer* with this endeavor.

But with Maribel departing for the Washington Nationals, we lacked one essential ingredient: a fourth teammate.

This is where we relied on *relationships*. I sent out an e-mail to various co-workers explaining our plight. Using my marketing thinking cap, I positioned it as a great opportunity to join an exciting and lively relay team!

The silence was deafening.

Joining a relay team is no small task and unless you really were searching for a workout program, or a new goal in life, people aren't going to jump at the opportunity. But K-Mad noticed one thing.

"It's obvious you're pumped about doing this," she noted one night early in the Padres season in Press Dining, our version of a staff cafeteria, "and so am I. What we need then isn't to excite another person but to attract a person that is *already* excited."

In walked Alison Glabe.

Alison coordinated operations for our group and season-tickets salespeople, a fairly straightforward and labor-intensive job. But apart from that she wrote a blog about Vera Bradley, a collection of colorful handbags and accessories, and radiated exuberance. She wasn't generally bubbly or perky, like a highly-caffeinated cheerleader, she was just excitable in general.

When something got her going, be it a "Vera sighting" or a ladybug landing on her shoe, then the excitement spilled forward. Like a stream of water she could gush words rapidly in run-on sentences and her e-mails often contained many exclamation marks!!!!

We invited her to join us for Press Dining dinner, which was always a solid meal during home games for the great price of five dollars. After the third inning they serve hot dogs for the even better price of zero dollars.

K-Mad explained our situation and said, "Alison, we are trying to show people that anything is possible! That a team of non-runners and one guy with a prosthetic leg can complete a marathon! As Alex says, "it's possible to achieve what others think is madness!"

"But I'm not a runner either!" Alison protested. "I think I would just slow you guys down."

Finally I stopped chewing my hot dog long enough to kick in the other aspect of relationships—not just knowing a person, but knowing *about* them.

"A.G.", I called her this because it was both her initials and our star first baseman's, Adrian González, "I'll make you a deal. I admit, we're desperate here. But it's more than that. We love your charisma and joy for life. You join our relay team…and I'll buy you a Vera Bradley bag."

It was like fireworks had exploded and angels sang. Alison smiled widely.

"Really?! Well, that might be bribery. But I'm in! I want to help you guys anyway but how can I resist a Vera bag? A.G. is in!"

Karen and I fist-bumped. K-Mad prepared to speak but Alison interjected. "I mean, I have done the Breast Cancer Three-Day walk, and that's really inspirational, and I imagine this race is really inspirational, especially with the mission you guys are on, and oh, I better start running, but I will, and…"

We now had our team assembled, but, ironically, the training was going to be delayed for about ten days. It was early April and the Padres had just completed a shaky first road trip and were returning for their first homestand of 2010.

A home opener is teeming with excitement and anticipation and for baseball staffers, work. It's the first curtain on Broadway combined with the first day of school. Everything has to be ready because fans have waited all winter to walk through those gates and when they do, they want to see a magnificent playing field, sparkling concourses, and banners bursting with color. Opening Day attracts so many visitors—generally it sells out—many of whom will base their decision to return on this first-game experience. Thus, we want Colbie Caillat to shine as a Grammy-Award-winning national anthem singer and for every ticket to be printed properly.

K-Mad was coordinating the pre-game entertainment for all of Opening Week (six games), Alison oversaw the ticket sales operations, and Colleen McEniry was distributing leather flight-style Padres jackets the club was giving to full season ticket holders. I didn't have much to do for that opener versus the Atlanta Braves, but five games later it would be Mexico Opening Night, our annual tribute to our Latino fans, which I coordinated.

We were all putting in long hours with great intensity, thereby reducing hours and energy for training. After the Braves and then Diamondbacks were leaving town, we could get back to early morning workouts for Colleen and Karen or early afternoon workouts for Alison and me.

Opening Day glimmered with hope. Caillat belted out the national anthem and as she did so, a burst of rain caused a Padres staffer to hold an umbrella over the heads of the singer and her guitarist. Then—true story—as soon as the patriotic song ended, the clouds parted and sunshine drenched beautiful Petco Park. I told K-Mad, who panicked when the first drop fell, that it was an omen about both the Padres and Team MADness: early storms followed by sunshine and warmth. She wasn't in the mood for feel-good stories. She wanted everything to go as scheduled, as planned, and with smooth efficiency. This applied to both her job and marathon training.

But it was true. After getting decked in Arizona and Colorado, we christened the home schedule, against a true powerhouse, the Braves, with a 17-2 victory. It was the most runs we had ever scored at Petco, and I think I set a new record for most bruises on Nick Golden's hand with constant fist bumps. More importantly, it was a reminder that early adversity need not flatten a person or team. What mattered was not how hard you got hit but how quickly you get back up.

More adversity came our way, though, along with grumbling that this was a repeat of the past two seasons, when Atlanta won the next two to take the series.

The Arizona Diamondbacks then came to our house and promptly started the weekend by jumping to a 4-0 lead on Friday night.

Then, some magic happened.

The lads chipped away and trimmed the lead to 4-3. Still, it was already the eighth inning on this foggy and chilly spring night and the prospect of falling to 3-7 hung like the damp air.

I was visiting some clients in our Omni Premiere Club lounge and had a good view of an unfortunate scene: people already trudging up the aisles in anticipation of a defeat. In the bottom of the ninth, a base hit occurred. Then another hit. Suddenly those that were filing out stood near the top of their sections.

Up to the plate stepped Chase Headley. I had admired Chase not only because he wore my favorite number on his jersey (seven) but because he had endured quite a bit in his young Padres career. From highly touted draftee and minor-league prospect (once being named the Texas League MVP) to someone who moved from third base to left field per the team's request, his future was cloudy. All winter he had been the subject of trade rumors.

I found it pleasantly ironic that I was viewing Chase's at-bat in the Omni Club because nearby was the Omni Hotel; there I had met him for the first time upon his call-up in 2008—we were both dining in the hotel restaurant—and was impressed with how unassuming and good-natured the former Tennessee Volunteer star was.

Crack! A fastball had just been blistered and the remaining, scattered crowd roared, making a sound similar to a cannon being shot. Number seven stood at home plate, watched the arc of his fly ball, and as his roundhouse swing was completed, kept his right wrist elevated as his bat fell to the ground. He looked like a basketball player who froze his movements while watching a deep three-pointer swish through the net.

The ball sailed through the cold night, its orbit causing it to land in the right-field bleachers. Whereas Headley looked calm and composed, transfixed at home plate, his swing caused delirium in the stands. A 4-3 deficit had just become a 6-4 triumph and fans and teammates were jumping around joyously.

I pumped my fist and breathed a sigh of relief. 4-6 sure looked much better than 3-7.

The momentum had carryover effect too, as the Padres won their next two in the weekend set. Suddenly the lads were a respectable 6-6 and confidence, along with solid pitching acumen, was growing.

I was more focused on getting back to marathon training. I trusted my teammates were doing the same but was more concerned with my performance; it was mid-April and I was still only completing about three or four laps in two hours. This was the equivalent of roughly two miles and I needed to double that.

I texted K-Mad, AG, and CoCo my nightly results and even when they didn't respond, it kept me accountable to them. We were keeping it F.R.E.S.H. and keeping it determined.

As April began to dissolve into warmer days and early evenings, the Padres moved into first place on the twentieth day of that month. Even with the increased warmth, there was enough of a chill when the sun set that it reminded me of happy times as an undergraduate at Notre Dame.

I pondered this spring nirvana, and the Padres early pole position, when I encountered that same fan I had seen at ticket windows on the first day of the season.

"Hey!" I greeted him as I lowered the volume on *Xavier the X-Man* deejaying on my old-school Walkman. "How 'bout them Padres, huh? They just moved into first place!"

"Don't get too excited," the man shot back, "it's early. It won't last. There's no way they'll have a winning record, let alone be contenders in the division."

I paused. Maybe the curmudgeon was right. It was early and there was plenty of time for this young team to come back to earth.

KNOW WHEN TO SACRIFICE

Cinco de Mayo brings annual festivities with margaritas, music, and mouth-watering Mexican food. In this year, 2010, it brought the realization that in exactly one month would be the San Diego Rock 'n' Roll Marathon race weekend. That meant we had four weeks to be in shape and, according to my personal plan I'd outlined, exceed what I was going to walk on race day so that it would seem easier.

I had made one key adjustment to my training regimen. Weeknights after work, when the Padres were on the road, I walked for two hours, which was usually amounting to about three miles in distance. I wasn't pleased but it seemed to be what my body was allowing.

So instead of beating myself up over that, I accepted those as tune-up sessions that were keeping me better-conditioned. On the weekends I would choose a Saturday or

Sunday, usually on a day when my friends were not enjoying the dance floors in Pacific Beach or East Village, and do longer walks. I was actually in the process of getting a new prosthetic leg (though it wouldn't be ready until after the race) so my current leg was old—I had worn it for twelve years—and heavy and not conducive to running, but I knew I could walk on it.

And I knew weekends would have to be where I really pushed myself to increase mileage and stamina and hopefully decrease some time.

Walking while wearing artificial limbs is, in general, not an easy proposition. Whichever type of prosthetic leg, be it one that connects to an amputee's hip or is mainly a below-the-knee socket if they have half of their limb still, it's essentially a piece of wood and/or graphite strapped to your hip. That causes you to lean into it or limp.

Those that have two artificial legs walk slightly stiff, with their upper torso usually moving quite a bit as the hips swivel. Someone like me with one prosthetic leg will lean to the right a lot while my good leg, on the left, absorbs all the pressure and weight from being the one natural leg.

Also, because I wear two prosthetic arms, that's about ten extra pounds to carry. I never really feel it, weight-wise, unless I am walking fast or for a long distance because then the weight of the arms with the weight of the prosthetic leg all seemingly wear on me. Too, endurance walking forces you to swing your arms back and forth so that your upper body is taking some pressure off your lower torso. When your arms are connected to you via a strap harness, as mine are, after two laps it is a real strain to keep those arms moving. The first one to complain, especially if I have not stretched properly, is my lower back.

With race day a month away, I allowed myself one night of Cinco de Mayo gorging, and then returned to better eating. Understand that I love food like a fish loves water. I'm not going to blame my parents, because some of my siblings are very trim. Growing up, I knew my brother Jorge and younger sister Ines were consistently thin, and my older sister Elizabeth and I more easily packed on the pounds. If they have a gene for loving candy, fried foods, and soda, I inherited it.

I also feel like food should be one of life's pleasures. Enjoy it! Like I told my co-worker and close friend Nina Tarantino, "I love bacon like I love babies."

I pride myself on honesty and being very real. The truth is I love to eat and frankly love lots of foods that are not high on nutritional value. I was not just going to give those up and be miserable.

But I could make some sacrifices. Although I really should have started earlier, for one month I crossed out the chocolates that were an afternoon staple. I love soda, especially Coca-Cola. I know it's not good for my belly or kidneys, but I enjoy it so much. Will I give it up? No. Will I drink a little less of it, opting for more juices and when I do clamor for soda, go for the diet variety? Yes.

Aside from Maribel, one of our other colleagues, John Turnour, had also gotten a job offer that spring with the Washington Nationals. On his final day with our marvelous grounds crew, a farewell happy hour was held in his honor.

This is where sacrifices, and specifically diligence, took hold. I said goodbye to John that day and thanked him for being a great friend and co-worker. That particular week was a busy one with a work commitment on Monday night (in my role I attend various mixers in the community), a speaking engagement on Wednesday night, and then Thursday we were starting a homestand.

I had one night to train because the Padres home games were going to wipe out my workouts, aside from a late Sunday afternoon walk and some weightlifting I could do at home. John completely understood and wished me luck. We both agreed we'd be staying in touch via e-mail and Facebook anyway.

So that Tuesday evening, I trotted around beautiful Petco Park's exterior, swinging my arms, stretching my neck to keep it loose, and keeping my legs moving. My cell phone in my shirt pocket kept buzzing and on occasional quick breaks I would glance at the text messages: *Where are you? You're missing a great party! Taco Tuesday here and the drinks are cheap!*

Man, I was tempted to cut my walk short or bail on it altogether. But I attempted to take a big-picture view. If I didn't walk tonight, I wouldn't be walking again until five days later at the earliest. The next week were home games, which eliminated training altogether. If I essentially missed two weeks, my next training day would be rusty and I'd probably need a day just to ease back into it; I know my body. Time was running short. June was creeping rapidly.

I shot a quick text back: *Sorry, Johnny knows I have to train tonight. Sad but true. Raise a toast in my absence.*

One point I'd like to add, though, is that although sacrifices must be made in the pursuit of excellence, you have to include reality and fun. Your goals must be realistic and you must keep having fun in order to achieve them.

Team MADness was working hard on our individual training regiments. During the day I was at least attempting to eat better. But at night, during the Padres home games, we'd have some fun. In the press dining room where we ate dinner, we allowed ourselves to splurge, not every night, naturally, but still quite a few. We grabbed hot dogs and tortilla chips and Karen and Alison would add chili beans to their dogs. All three girls added cheese to their chips, but not me because I can't stand cheese. It disgusts me.

Nina and Nick would enter after their work shifts ended and see our monstrous plates of chili cheese dogs, hot dogs, nacho chips, and the occasional brownie or bowl of ice cream.

"What," they would ask in unison, "are you guys eating?"

One or all of us would then respond: "Tee Matness Raining Die."

When one's mouth is not full of food that translates to: Team MADness Training Diet.

You have to be different from the norm. You have to make sacrifices. But you have to keep it fun. Isn't that what this is all about?

I DON'T KNOW
IF I CAN DO THIS

Night after night, as soon as I was done with my workday, I would open the glass doors of our front lobby at 100 Park Boulevard. The downtown condominiums had a late spring breeze swirl through their walkways and in between the buildings. Each week more residents seemed to be coming out for jogs at sunset.

I made a personal rule that my cell phone could come on my training sessions but had to stay firmly entrenched in my shirt pocket. It could only be removed if I had some sort of emergency or mishap. I also had my antiquated Walkman but because fiddling to find a good song was slowing me down, I picked one station each night and stayed on it.

Team MADness was slumping. Alison was loathing running. Colleen was finding it hard to balance training with two jobs. K-Mad was getting excited about race day in three weeks but after each session noticed her knees feeling sore.

I was struggling. My stamina had increased and I was up to five or six laps of the three-quarters-of-a-mile perimeter of beautiful Petco Park. But despite the sweat and increased pace and push to keep moving forward, one thing was missing—speed. I could walk four to five miles now but it would take me close to three hours. That rate would wreck our agreed-upon budgeted times and leave us at risk of getting picked up by the "straggler shuttles."

My mind was constantly in overdrive. Working in baseball means: handling ticket requests, reviewing letters asking for autograph items, coordinating events, and always worrying about your team's performance. To us, that team is a love and a business. We pour our hearts into following and working for them.

As an amputee I'm always thinking about stretching; not exerting too much pressure on the prosthetic leg; ensuring the waist strap doesn't break; keeping my neck and shoulders loose where the arms' strap harness hangs on them; and not twisting or placing too much weight on my one good foot.

So as I'm walking and trying to decrease my times, I'm thinking about everything from coordinating my torso movements to coordinating the Padres Cinco de Mayo Celebration.

Working out, though, helps your mind as much as your body. The magical thing about walking or jogging is that you think about all these things and then they kind of leave you, like sweat coming out of your pores. I would think through all my problems and some nights a solution would appear and some nights the solution was just thinking it over and deciding to attack it tomorrow. Either way your mind gets refreshed.

By the middle of May the Padres were neck and neck with our longtime nemesis, the Los Angeles Dodgers, for first place. It was early but excitement was building with each win. When the Dodgers came to town for a weekend set it was our first taste of a big series in about four years.

Dodger fans were pumped, Padres fans were hyped, and the weekend tilt coincided with our launch of a partnership with national organization *Stand Up To Cancer*. Before the Friday opener we held a press conference where Padres manager Bud Black and Dodgers skipper Joe Torre helped unveil some portable walls fans could sign in remembrance of loved ones touched by cancer.

As solemn as that type of press conference was, there was a buzz as well. The media arrived in throngs and the presser featured actor Ray Liotta, a personal favorite of mine from 1990s mob classic "Goodfellas." As spokesperson he emphasized this was a groundbreaking partnership and a time to rejoice!

Team MADness set aside our training for the weekend because we all had to work the Dodgers series and sellout crowds each game meant about 120,000 fans would be pouring through the turnstiles.

The excited and loud fans came. The Padres offense did not.

The Dodgers won Friday, Saturday, and Sunday—a three-game sweep that knocked us out of first place. We looked so bad.

As the sun set on Sunday, the three consecutive losses in the books, Karen Madden plopped into a chair in front of my desk. "This weekend can just suck it," she said.

"I know," I responded dejectedly, "we got beat pretty soundly. I don't know if we can stay in this pennant race."

"Not just that," Karen said while rubbing her knee. "My knee will not stop hurting and I'm starting to limp like you!"

We both laughed but I was concerned. K-Mad appeared injured and we didn't know how or to what extent.

My mind flashed back to four nights earlier, the Thursday evening before the series, when I did a few laps around the ballpark as workers readied it for play and, in our Palm Court Promenade, the cancer awareness press conference. I bumped into Robert Davis, our Inside Sales supervisor, who took a break from his workout to watch the cancer-message walls being erected.

"What do you think, R.D.?" I inquired between breaths. "Can we win this series?"

In his quiet and measured tone Robert said, "I think so. But, bro, you have to remember, it's a marathon. We have to stay humble and focused and just stay in the race."

He could've been talking about the Rock 'n' Roll but specifically he meant the pennant race. That weekend we were humbled. The Padres and Team MADness were teams clouded in doubt that needed an infusion of strategy and confidence.

"We need to get off to a good start but in order to do that we should have someone who is fast but more importantly has endurance because early on it's going to be packed, and the second leg not so much but that's on the freeway, and I do *not* want to be that person. a.m. is going fourth so maybe I should just go third."

That was Alison. She spoke as she thought, each phrase a twist and serpentine turn of emotions, doubts, confirmations, and added thoughts.

"What if I kick off the race and Colleen, you go second?" Karen said. "Neither one really is ideal but I'll be pretty fired up having all the other racers around me and your leg is a long one, but it's early so there should still be a cloud cover."

Karen was always very even-keeled in her explanation, perhaps owing to her degree in Education and background as a teacher, and role as Padres Entertainment Coordinator, juggling national anthem singers, clowns who make balloons, celebrities throwing First Pitches, and more.

Colleen shrugged. "That's cool with me."

That was a great thing about Colleen. She was the shortest among us and could be tough and feisty in her own right, but only when something really set her off. Otherwise she was generally very mellow, which made you notice and respect the louder moments when they did occur.

Team MADness was seated at a gray, metallic table at Lolita's at the Park, the small Mexican restaurant just across the street from Petco Park. The Rock 'n' Roll Marathon was roughly three weeks away and we had to move from slumping team to a smart and well-orchestrated one.

Likewise, I noticed as I put down my copy of the *San Diego Union-Tribune* sports page, Padres manager Bud Black said the sweep by the Dodgers showed him where he needed to maximize certain elements of his team. Specifically, it was a team short on power but long on pitching, bullpen depth, and team speed. His club, he confidently said, would rebound and win consistently by playing small-ball and emerging triumphant in low-scoring games.

"Put down that paper—we need to focus!" Karen snatched the newspaper from my hooks, not rudely but firmly. I smiled because I knew she was doing me a favor. I prided myself on the fact that, as someone in his mid-thirties, I still favored reading an actual newspaper whereas most of my younger colleagues received their news online. I like the crisp sound of pages turning and the high volume of content online news sites often lack.

But Karen was my age so I knew she wasn't trying to call me out as someone stuck in archaic times, though she did poke fun at my Walkman. She knew, and I could tell Alison and Colleen agreed because they laughed, that I could become so absorbed in the sports section I could tune out whatever conversation was being held. This particular conversation was about marathon planning.

My good friend from graduate school, Colleen McDonald, had sent a map of the marathon course with an e-mail detailing how many miles each leg of the race featured. As a registration coordinator for the race's parent company, Competitor Group International, she knew all aspects of the course, from distances to diversity—where it would be flat, or hilly, or hot, or cloudy, or packed, or vast with space.

"Don't forget, A-Mo," she wrote, using the nickname many called me, inspired by New York Yankees slugger Alex "A-Rod" Rodriguez, "I think your best bet is to go last and you guys *have* to finish in seven hours."

"Colleen is right," Alison said, referring to McDonald, "the map shows that the final leg is from Mission Bay Park to Fiesta Island, which is fairly flat, plus the sun might be going down, which should help you stay cool, because we don't need you wearing down because I for one am NOT getting picked up by a shuttle, especially with all this training I'm doing, plus you're getting me a Vera bag, so we're going to finish and finish strong! Oh and I'll take the leg before yours, that's no problem."

Whenever Alison would go on one of these speaking jags, which was often, K-Mad and I would just look at each other in stunned disbelief. How does someone say so many words without catching her breath?

The Colleen that was sitting with us at Lolita's, our teammate McEniry, pushed aside her tray and started scribbling some notes.

"Ok, let's work backwards," she said, "and figure this out. Alex has acknowledged that flat terrain and more time will help him because of his prosthetic leg. So he'll go last and Alison, you'll run right before him?"

"I sure wiiiillll!" AG also punctuated her more enthusiastic comments with a sing-song melody and by dragging out certain words.

McEniry continued, "So that means the longest legs of the race really will be the first two. I feel like I'm fairly fast because I'm the shortest, so why don't I do the second leg? That's the stretch on Freeway 163 and there is nothing to see in terms of scenery, so whoever does it will want to be done quickly."

"That's a good idea…Hmmm, these nachos are yummy," Karen replied. "And really, with my knee hurting, I don't feel like speed is my best asset. So maybe that first leg is best for me because it's at dawn, which sounds, uh, terrible, but I'm sure the crowd at the starting line will get me excited. Plus that part is mostly through downtown so I can last those five miles."

"How is your knee?" I interjected. "You've been saying it hurts for a couple weeks now."

"Oh it does," Karen asserted, "but I don't think anything's going to solve it. I know nothing's broken. It's just really sore after I run. But, hey, we've come too far to just give up."

"That's the spirit!" Alison said cheerfully while laughing.

We had figured out our greatest needs and how to combat those with our strengths. To wit: Karen had a bum knee but a penchant for adrenaline rushes and she liked to set the tone in things. McEniry was roughly five foot two and in softball and other sports, she proved to be swift. Alison just had this zest for life and could occupy her mind for long stretches with thoughts of Vera bags. I write that half-kiddingly; as a veteran of the Susan G. Komen Three-Day Walks for Breast Cancer she had experience, stamina, and mental toughness to get through a grueling race.

And me, my greatest enemies were the three prosthetics weighing me down because my other enemy was time and our need to finish this thing in no more than seven hours. But I had faith it could be done; determination to keep practicing each night; and a plan to continually increase my mileage so that by June 6, I could walk four miles easily.

That was how we divided it:

Leg 1–Karen, nine miles
Leg 2–Colleen, seven miles

Leg 3–Alison, six miles
Leg 4–Alex, four miles

That totaled approximately twenty-six miles and we were pumped now that we had a plan.

We became even more hyped as June rolled in like the marine layer on San Diego Bay. The Friday before the race all participants were to pick up their registration packets at the San Diego Convention Center. AG, McEniry, and I walked over with our buddies Nina Tarantino, Krystal DiStefano, and Katie Leisz, who also were running individually, to the Convention Center just a block from beautiful Petco Park.

The shrill yells of cheerleaders and excited runners and walkers filled the glass building, and a makeshift red carpet was laid out to enter the expo hall. With the cheerleaders shrieking, and Alison snapping pictures behind me, I led our crew through a wall of pom-poms as I danced and raised my arms exultantly. My teammates rolled their eyes. I frequently winked mine.

Colleen McDonald greeted us and made sure we had our packets, including a drummer's drumstick as the baton. There was noise and racing gear for sale everywhere, like Las Vegas meets a bazaar.

"Good luck Sunday!" Coll said.

After an energy-infused hour we returned to work, and as we crossed Harbor Drive onto our work residence of 100

Park Boulevard, the one person that could not come to the race expo with us, showed up.

It was Karen. She had text-messaged us to go ahead because she could go later and wanted her doctor to see her first.

Now she was limping across the crosswalk and was wearing a knee brace.

"Oh my god!" Alison said it but we all thought it.

"Hi," Karen said softly. "So this is the deal. Apparently I have badly torn knee ligaments from all my running. My doctor said he's surprised my knee has held up this long and gave me this brace to keep it stable. It's been hurting, but mostly is sore, and wants me to see how I feel tomorrow. I told him if I can walk Saturday, I'm doing the race Sunday. But guys, I don't know if I can do this."

As Karen explained this, she teetered on a curb, perhaps mindlessly. Suddenly, she shifted her weight and almost fell over, before getting caught by her boyfriend Ken.

"Whoaaa!" we exclaimed simultaneously.

We laughed at the sudden near-accident before Nina piped in, "Injured team leader hurts knee *and* sprains ankle. Now *that's* MADness!"

Everyone laughed at her usage of our team slogan and the tension was thankfully broken. We knew the gravity of the situation but Team MADness had this characteristic: we knew when to laugh. We knew when to plan, and get serious, and even had a couple people ready as extreme emergency back-ups in case injury (or illness) occurred.

But most important we knew to never lose our sense of humor.

It all hinged on how Karen felt in the morning. Now *this* was MADness.

JUST GET ME THERE

That same day that we registered, there was a high level of intense nerves, ranging from pre-race jitters to excitement. The Pads were in Philadelphia so the Friday afternoon work responsibilities were lessened, which allowed our relay team to marvel over the jerseys we had ordered to show solidarity. We wanted to prove that anything was possible with faith and teamwork, even an undertaking of madness like four novices, including a triple amputee, running a marathon.

So why not stand out in neon green jerseys with *Team Madness* emblazoned across the chest? Mine had a pocket stitched onto the front because I use shirt pockets to more easily pull out any belongings. "KMAD" on Karen Madden's, "AG" on Alison Glabe's, "COCO" on Colleen McEniry's, and "AMO" on mine.

We were still nervous about Karen's knee situation but excited that in less than forty-eight hours we were going to be in a marathon after months of training. Our co-workers

Katie Leisz, Krystal DiStefano, Danny Waite, and Jeff Brown were also running, so we chatted rambunctiously with them.

That night I knew I didn't want to just sit at home—which I rarely did on a weekend night anyway but especially with this amount of bundled-up energy—so I wanted to hit an establishment or two in the East Village. Obviously a full workout this close to race day would only sap me of strength but perhaps a little dancing would keep my legs strong and agile? Hey, I'm always looking for a reason to dance.

So I rounded up my best buds "Slick" Nick Golden, Shawn Rossi, and Alex Aguilar and we rolled to Fleetwood, a lounge on the corner of Seventh and J Street, where in the early evening hours they serve up beef skewers and string fries; later they serve up beats as they push away the furniture and install a DJ. You have to know when to break some conventional rules and have fun and we were doing that.

Midway through the night, my Fist Pumping was interrupted by a tap on my shoulder. It was Heather Contreras, fianceé of our work colleague Logan Washburn. She was there with her roommates as part of a girl's night out. I felt bad because I always remembered the name of one really cute roommate but would inevitably forget the others. It was like having Gladys Knight and the rest were Pips. No offense, ladies, men are pigs.

Heather was not only a good friend but a fellow devout Notre Dame football fan, so she normally greeted me enthusiastically. She did this time too, interrupting my best "Dougie" pop-and-lock move, but then extending her arms outward in confusion.

"Aren't you doing a *marathon* on Sunday?" she asked.

She pointed at the beer in my hand.

Laughing, I replied, "Hey, it's one beer. I'll be okay, just dancing for a couple hours."

I then leaned in and asked, "Now what are your roommates' names again?"

She punched me in the shoulder.

Slick Nick and Rossi wanted to call it an early night, and not too long after they departed, I left as well while Aguilar stayed behind. Before grabbing a taxi home I needed to stop by my desk at Petco, a couple blocks away, and started walking in that direction.

"Hey, man, why don't you have any hands?"

The person shouting was standing on a street corner and after I calmly stated that I was born without my arms, he peppered me with more questions. "How do you use the bathroom? You ever scratch someone's eye out with those things?"

I never mind, even in my worst moods, if someone approaches me and asks if they can ask a few questions. I'll answer any inquiry and unless I'm rushed to get somewhere, will generally answer politely. If you have the guts to ask me a question, I'll answer it. But don't just start spouting personal questions, without first asking me if it's cool to do so, and then doing it loudly so your Abercrombie and Fitch-wearing, bleached jeans-sporting cronies can laugh nearby.

My only escape was a pedicab driver on the same corner. He already had two female passengers but gave me a knowing look of wanting to rescue me from this East Coast-accented loudmouth.

I climbed in and one of the girls says, "I never seen arms like that before. Can I ask what happened?"

This approach felt far more dignified and genuine. So I explained about my birth defects and asked if they were from San Diego.

"No, baby, we from Boston!" she said while patting her chest. "We're in town to do the Rock 'n' Roll Marathon."

When I informed her that I was a local but was also participating in the same race, she exclaimed, "For real? Good for you!"

Grabbing my face with both hands she planted a kiss squarely on my lips. The pedicab driver pulled up to 100 Park Boulevard and I pulled some cash out of my shirt pocket, which I handed to him in a daze.

The next afternoon, after a day of fitful rest, I got dressed in slacks and a collared shirt. An organization in town called Hispanic Arts Theatre, which provided theatrical showcases for Hispanic actors and playwrights, had asked if they could present an award for support given to them by myself and the Padres. Not only was I hesitant because supporting them was just a natural and enjoyable aspect of my job, but I explained to them that I had to be up at 5:00 a.m. for the marathon.

Still, they persisted that this Annual Dinner was their largest fundraiser of the year and they promised if I came they'd allow me to slip out as soon as the program ended. So I relented and traded my mesh shorts and sneakers for pants and dress shoes.

It was also a sacrifice in that attending this function meant missing out on a dinner my teammates were having to "carbo load"—consume as much pasta and spaghetti in order to have carbohydrates in their system to keep their energy level high while running. This was standard practice for runners and even in all the years I was not involved in this race, the night before the Rock 'n' Roll meant San Diego's Italian restaurants were filled. My relay teammates were meeting up with Katie Leisz for a carbo-loading dinner and I was sorry to miss out.

As I was getting ready for the banquet I was attending, thinking of the team bonding my girls would enjoy, my cell phone started buzzing violently. Multiple text messages were coming in simultaneously. A quick glance of the inbox showed me that Karen sent a text, followed by her now-fianceé Ken, followed by Colleen McEniry, and finished up with a message from Alison.

From K-Mad: "My doctor says I have 'jumpers knee'… torn cartilage from excessive pounding…but I'm cleared to run the race!"

From Ken: "Karen has an effed up knee but she's all good. See you tomorrow, kid."

From Colleen: "Did Madden text u? Her doc sez she will b fine."

From Alison: "OMG! So excited! Karen's knee is pretty bad but her doctor is letting her run, and then she'll have to ice it and rehab it but she's in for the race!!!!!"

That last one took up two text messages.

I was thrilled that K-Mad was cleared to run. She had said she could endure one more day of pain and then look into some long-term solutions for her knee problem. We had some emergency runners lined up but, frankly, it wouldn't have been the same. We'd practiced and trained and pushed each other for months, and not only was this our team's namesake, but Karen was that veteran, respected leader every team in any sport or business needs. As if we weren't already excited our entire team felt an adrenaline boost that evening.

I went across town to the Hispanic Arts Theatre dinner, which was held in a restaurant that doubled as a performance venue for salsa and tango dancers and singers. The banquet was classy and the attendees extremely friendly, and more than once I shielded nearby guests from seeing my phone; my teammates were texting me pictures of their delicious-looking pasta meals and writing things like, "Boooo! Another plaque for your wall? Plaques can Suck It!"

A few lessons occurred to me as well, besides the fact that laughing out loud at texts will draw quizzical looks from people nearby (K-Mad had written "He doesn't deserve it!" in anticipation of Hispanic Arts Theatre presenting me a plaque). Although I was nervously glancing at my watch, sometimes you have to just let time pass, be at ease, and let events flow. The organizers knew I'd be departing early; why appear nervous and fidgety and risk not enjoying the moment, while also appearing ungrateful and uptight?

Once I committed to being serene I appreciated the kind words the hosts were saying in presenting my award. Though I didn't know, I'd be asked to give an acceptance speech. By allowing myself to be immersed in the moment, I just spoke from my heart, saying that it was a privilege supporting organizations like theirs because I felt a connection to my Colombian roots, and also that they were the embodiment of American idealism by faithfully pursuing their dreams. With a spotlight beaming upon me that made the audience invisible and made me feel like my beads of sweat were illuminated, I explained that whether you are an actor, or singer, or entrepreneur, or aspiring marathoner, one should not be afraid to take risks and that in life you must always, always swing for the fences.

Graciously, they stood and applauded, over two hundred arts patrons whistling and cheering. Even as I struggled to make my way to the exits for my agreed-upon early departure, I maintained that just-go-with-it attitude and innate peace as people stopped to offer congratulations. I am glad too because, among the many kind people I encountered, one of them was a lady by the name of Ana Reyes. Ana was in charge of Spanish-language media relations at SONY and her Colombian husband, Juan, headed up the local Colombian Chamber of Commerce. Meeting them was one of those moments where you knew a wonderful friendship had just been kindled.

There was one more moment where an attitude of calm needed to be displayed, specifically sixty moments.

The dinner organizers, after a warm goodbye, ordered me a taxi so I could get home and get some much-needed rest. Of course, the taxi driver got lost as the restaurant was in a remote corner of Pacific Beach and a fifteen minute wait turned into thirty-five, which turned into sixty. *Serenity now, serenity now.*

I figured getting upset would make me even more tired eventually, so I made the most, invoked my "What's Important Now?" mantra, and socialized with more guests. I made more friends that way and remained calm and at peace. Finally after almost seventy-five minutes of waiting, mostly while standing, my cab arrived.

I got home, checked my Facebook, saw that my teammates had posted more "Too bad you missed our dinner, Mr. Big Time" messages on my Wall, and then reclined for a sleep

I knew would be antsy because my adrenaline, nerves, and emotions were all sky-high.

By the time I started drifting off it was nearly 1:00 a.m. I had to be up at five.

Race day had finally arrived.

RACE DAY.
KEEP PUSHING.

Sunday, June 6, 2010.

The pre-dawn hours gave way to a terse, gray light as morning was shrouded by a layer of clouds that hung low. I had set my cell phone as my alarm clock because I was waking up a good hour-and-a-half earlier than a normal workday but even the beeps of the alarm proved inconsequential. Four hours' sleep really was not too low because my anticipation of the marathon made it difficult to lie still anyway.

The most important thing was how my legs felt, both my good left one, and half right one that every day I slid into a prosthetic made of a composite of wood, fiberglass, and foam. As I strapped the Velcro belt around my waist, making sure it felt secure but not too tight, I was pleased that my legs felt fairly fresh. My hips felt fresh too because when you walk with a prosthetic leg your hips and lower back work harder to compensate for the missing limb.

The previous Sunday I put myself through one final rigorous walk in the Paradise Hills neighborhood of San Diego. That is the outlying area where I live and the immediate area in which our cul-de-sac resides is called Skyline Hills. Both names are appropriate because there are plenty of hills, not tremendously steep ones like in San Francisco, but arcing high enough that in the distance Skyline Hills has a view of the Pacific Ocean and Paradise Hills has a vantage point of downtown. That sun-splashed day the Padres had beaten the Washington Nationals in extra innings, so with the excitement of an extra-innings victory and the knowledge that the race was in seven days, I walked approximately four miles.

During the week I went on two very brief walks, about one and a half miles each, to keep my stamina sharp but otherwise rested my wheels. It was 5:00 a.m. now and I was wide awake.

It's important in any sport to know your body but especially when you wear prosthetics. For me, knowing that wearing my *gear* adds extra weight, I've learned that every workout requires a large amount of stretching. So from the minute I strapped on my leg I started stretching my back, neck, and left leg. I rotated my left foot to get blood flowing and get it loose. I twisted and turned to prepare my hips.

Equally important was stretching my mind. I was nervous about the daunting day ahead. Continuously I reminded myself that I trained for the last six months and nothing was going to be different today except instead of walking solo, there would be thousands of legs running near me.

Another aspect of being a person with a disability in general, and a prosthetics-wearer in particular, is I'm always thinking two steps ahead. My mind is trained on potential things in which I may need assistance or potential pratfalls in independent tasks, transportation, or mobility.

For example, knowing that I would need some help pinning my race bib onto my neon-green jersey, I asked Mama to be up by 5:30 a.m. (on a Sunday no less) to help me with that and lacing up my Adidas sneakers. After tucking my Team MADness jersey into my blue mesh shorts, which had gold "ND" emblazoned near the left pocket and the word "IRISH" across the back left, I thought ahead to transportation. Knowing all freeways were closed, negating any opportunity for anyone to give me a ride, I relied on my usual mode of public transportation. Which meant I gave myself twenty minutes to scarf a bowl of cereal in order to hop on a bus. That bus would take me to a trolley station downtown. After hopping on a trolley, I'd ride it to the Mission Bay section of town where my relay spot was located.

Always think two steps ahead in timing, relationships, decisions, finances, and attitude. I am glad I did because a mere block from the trolley station on the intersection of Imperial and Twelfth Avenue, the bus driver announced that that intersection was officially part of the race course so no traffic was permitted.

I looked at my phone and sure enough, Karen had sent a text about how pumped she was to be at the starting line with tens of thousands of runners and that she would soon be running past Petco Park and the nearby Imperial trolley stop. This was great, I thought, but how did our local Metropolitan Transit System not post advance notifications that certain bus or trolley stations were off-limits due to the race?

Those of us on city transit bus route eleven were then scurried onto another bus, where there were already passengers, and that bus went around the back edge of downtown to another trolley stop on Fifth Avenue and C Street. Think of it as getting to your driveway, turning right, and driving around the entire neighborhood in order to reach your house again. But life is all about making the most of any situation so instead of stewing about this nuisance, I chatted up the people on this second shuttle. Three people nearest to me were from Indiana, Texas, and New York either running today or cheering on runners. The Texan, from San Antonio, was a member of Team in Training and running in memory of a brother she lost to cancer.

After bonding with these folks, and providing as much local knowledge as I could about navigating the city (making me feel suddenly grateful for this re-route), I hopped on the red trolley to Morena Boulevard about twenty minutes away. Checking the texts on my phone, Karen was completing her route, on by what now had to be a pained knee, while McEniry was starting hers. I knew I was in the general vicinity of Mission Bay Park—where Alison was to pass me the drum stick/baton—but had almost two hours until then.

And I was still hungry and knew lunch would not be a possibility. So how about a second breakfast? What's in this strip mall nearby? Ooooh, pizza!

A half-hour later, after a slice of pizza and bottle of water, I walked back to the trolley station, knowing that Mission Bay Park was within distance of there. I saw a race official and asked him where the shuttles were to deposit racers to the park.

Gruffly he responded, "There ain't no shuttles! You gotta walk there."

"I don't like that answer and I really don't like your attitude, Mr. Mustachioed Race Official. Good day, sir," I said. "Good day!"

What choice did I have but to stretch, say another prayer, smile, at him and at God, and start walking on Sea World Drive toward my starting point on Mission Bay Park? The clouds were beginning to burn off and a stream of sunshine was pouring through. It was pleasant now at 10:00 a.m. but soon it was bound to get hot.

I had ensured Mama slathered me in sunscreen, which increasingly seemed like a wise decision. I tugged at my blue

Padres cap, smiled at those around me staring at my leg, and knew I had some walking to do. My leg of the race would be approximately four miles. To get to my relay spot I now had to walk two miles.

Sea World Drive, which connects the 8 Freeway to one of San Diego's most famous tourist and family destinations, slopes upwards and then retreats onto a downward tilt as it reaches Mission Bay Park. I tried to ignore the reality that hills are a harder workout—even downhill because I then place more weight on my left leg in order to maintain my balance—by perpetually looking at my telephone. Texts from well-wishers were streaming in.

From Slick Nick: "Good luck, buddy! Tear it up today so I can buy you a beer!"

From Rossi: "Have a blessed race, bud, I'm proud of you."

From my collegiate mentor Bob Mundy in South Bend:" Alejandro, thinking of you today on your marathon. Don't get arrested. Go Irish!"

From my buddy Adriana Holguin: "Pace yourself–Martin, the kids, and I are proud of you!"

From my brother-in-law Dean: "Ann and I are proud of you, brother. Go get 'em!"

These messages gave me a real lift as I trudged up that hill. I reminded myself to walk slowly because I needed to conserve energy and didn't want to pull any muscles either. At the apex of the hill a stream of runners came toward me, the only thing separating us was the yellow freeway lines. At this stage of the morning, a good three hours after the gun had sounded and tens of thousands shot out of the starting gates, those doing the full or half-marathon were already well into the race.

Alison sent me a text saying Colleen had already taken off and was due to reach her within the hour. My stomach was knotting up but I knew it was too early to be truly nervous. Instead of fretting about my speed or endurance, what was important now? Stretching. Staying hydrated. Staying loose while resting.

I located a table where community volunteers laid out cups of water and orange slices.

Grabbing water and sitting on a concrete bench, I realized I wasn't truly tired but had definitely lost any sort of freshness or bounce to my legs on that two-mile hike.

I was learning more about racing culture too. A runner reached the park and yelled out, "On on!" No one answered. He jogged a few more yards. Again he shouted. "On on!"

This time a couple on the grassy side of the knoll shouted back, "On on! Right here! Right here!"

They then handed the runner, who was drenched in sweat, a bottle of beer. He stopped, swigged the beer, high-fived them, and resumed running.

Noticing my stare, the provider of the beer, who sported a t-shirt reading Running Club of Long Beach, offered me a beer.

"What?" I replied, taken aback. "Oh, no thanks, man. I think I'd just get even thirstier."

He grinned and said, "No problem" and looked for more people to which he and his wife could give beers.

These runners are crazy! What a new world this was to me.

After about an hour, as I continually squatted, stretched, and moved around to keep my muscles active, Alison sent a text: "On way! Be ready!"

My word, I thought, *she's somehow texting while running!*

I hadn't kept too close a watch on time but figured everyone on Team MADness was running at their prescribed times because Alison was reaching me right as we had estimated–noon sharp.

I then thought about my personal time. My adrenaline was flowing as expected and based on my most recent training sessions, I just hoped to walk my four miles in three hours. If I could get a boost of energy as we neared the finish line in the parking lot of Sea World, two hours and forty-five minutes seemed attainable. Anything less than that was probably a truly mad notion.

Standing at the highest point of Mission Bay Park, which sloped downward and then ran parallel to the freeway, I watched as runners passed their drumstick to the next person on their relay team. Unlike an Olympic or competitive event, there was no great hurry or intense second where a dropped baton is devastation, because those running for cash prizes and such were way ahead anyway. This allowed for Alison to call out in a singsong voice, "I'm heeere! Ooh, let me walk with you!"

I laughed and hugged AG. She seemed a bit surprised but I just wanted to express my gratitude for her joining our team and constant enthusiasm throughout.

This was it. Sometimes you think about the big moments in your life, anticipating them so intently, and they arrive softly and simply. My stretching was complete and true, my legs weren't as fresh as expected because of the two-mile pre-walk, but now I needed to focus on the other FRESH–Faith, Relationships, Energy, Staying Connected, Hit a Homer.

It was go time.

Alison pointed out that her parents were nearby and before we started walking, her mother snapped a quick picture of us. Alison then took a picture of me with her phone, my arms raised exultantly, and uploaded it immediately onto Facebook. Within seconds, Colleen McDonald, working near the finish line, pressed "Like".

I was on my way, Alison by my side for half a mile, and when concrete intersected with gravel, on my own.

Right away, there was a challenge. The streets sloped, and I could feel myself tilting to the left. My left leg was naturally bearing all the weight and my muscles in my back and lower right side were tilting. A combination of adrenaline and the slope was causing me to walk rather fast.

Every single time I trained in the six months prior, I noticed that if I started out too quickly, inevitably my lower back muscles would tighten into a knot. Conversely, if I started slow and picked up speed the further I went, my longevity was much better.

I felt a bit of panic. What if I trained all these months and had to stop because of muscle tightness? I would be letting so many people down! Heck, *I'd* feel let down!

So I stopped and regained my calmness. I stretched out once more, and I resumed walking at a slower pace. Sometimes in life, you just need to stop, calm your nerves, and start over.

A young lady in a pink tank top, just as I was picking up speed, came from behind and asked if I'd take a picture with her. I said yes but must have looked pretty confused because she said, as if to explain, "You're very inspirational!"

I responded, "You're hot!" She grinned and dashed away.

There was no looking back now. I had four miles on Fiesta Island, which connected Mission Bay Park to Sea World, to walk in less than three hours.

My focus was so intense at the outset that I was a bit startled by a noise I heard as I began my walk: hands clapping. People lined up in two columns to cheer on the walkers and runners, much like cheerleaders forming a wall as a football team charges out of the tunnel. When they spotted me, specifically my arms and artificial leg, they graciously applauded. Aside from the Glabes, no one knew who I was, of course, so what I heard was: "All right, Team MADness! Let's go Team MADness!"

If they saw the name on the back of my jersey, it was humorous because there was no room for a hyphen in A-Mo. Therefore what they saw was *AMO* and their shouts were, "Let's go Ammo! Way to go, Ammo!"

I never before had heard my nickname pronounced like artillery.

Aside from that quirk, the cheers really were helpful. Perhaps they presumed that I was a war veteran or had lost my limbs in an accident. It didn't matter. The cheers and whistles were genuine and Ammo felt pumped.

Sailing through the first stretch, I easily reached the fork in the road where half and full-marathoners went left and relay teams went right. It was a smartly-designed marathon course.

An older gentleman, who apparently was not part of the race, steered his bicycle toward me and pedaled right alongside as I walked. He didn't say anything but merely smiled. I felt this was a bit unusual but even that emotion gave way to curiosity about what he had on his handlebars: two American flags on wooden sticks.

Noticing my gaze, the man asked, "Would you like a flag? I only need one."

"Yeah, man," I answered, "I would."

And that's how I acquired an American flag to carry the rest of the way. My patriotic pride was swelling.

We were stepping onto Fiesta Island now, which if it was as flat as advertised, based on the curve I had just completed, should make for a relatively easy walk. My heart rate seems normal and I'm barely perspiring. This should be pretty easy!

I declined the first couple of tables I saw on the side of the road manned by volunteers holding plastic cups of water. Those popped up every one hundred feet or so but I liked my pace and did not want to stop.

A lady was walking her poodle near me and then beside me and started eyeing my prosthetics. I prepared for any questions she might ask about how my arms worked and such. She then blurted out, "So what the hell happened to you?"

Deciding I didn't have time for her lack of grace or her poodle, I said, "Sorry, can't talk, gotta go." Picking up the pace, I left her behind.

Cotton-mouth—when your mouth gets appreciably drier—was starting to set in. But what I was noticing were the Team in Training t-shirts all around me from various cities. Chicago. Miami. NYC. Some inscribed messages onto their shirts or arms. *Running for you, Mom. Dedicated to Patty. This is for Frank. Scotty, Isabelle, Megan.*

The mood, though, was invariably upbeat. I could hear the sounds of the first Rock 'n' Roll band, which were placed on stages at seemingly every half mile, just up ahead. But around me people were shouting exhortations. Some were aimed at me. Others were for Team in Training members, which raised funds for cancer research. I also saw people who ran not to set personal marks but to exclusively encourage first time runners. *You can do it! Looking great! Doing great!*

One cheer stayed with me: *Keep pushing now!*

An hour elapsed. I allowed myself glances at my watch but despite its incessant humming, kept my cell phone in my shirt pocket. Alison had told me she'd inform Karen and Colleen (plus our buddies Nina, Krystal, and Katie) that I was off and, well, walking so I knew I didn't have to reach out to them.

At an hour-and-a-half, I stopped for some water and a quick rest. Then I resumed walking. My brisk pace was slowing. This is where I felt the culmination of the unanticipated two-mile walk. My legs felt heavier. My pace was slowing.

Whenever I walk anywhere with friends I know that, based on their having two legs to my one, I'm going to eventually fall to the back of the pack. I almost always bring up the rear and if I wasn't in last place now I knew I had to be one of the final ones.

As the crowd of runners and walkers thinned out, there was far more spacing. The cheers at the park were a distant memory and all that could be heard now was heavy breathing and sneakers hitting pavement and gravel. It was getting warmer. I was growing thirstier. The quietness seemed to increase and it was almost a surreal individual experience.

Ahead of me I could see a bend that showed runners seemingly miles ahead. They looked so far ahead.

Occasionally we'd reach signs that read "Only three miles left!" *Three miles? I feel like I've already walked three and there should be one left!*

Could I do this? I never seriously contemplated giving up but that doesn't mean my confidence was high. My legs felt heavier, my hips were barely turning…must…keep… pushing.

What did I get myself into? Even if I do make it all the way can I make it in time for MADness to achieve the seven-hour goal? I can't do this. Why am I out here?

"Hey, Irish!"

Oh gosh. Every time I heard that it was someone with a USC shirt or Michigan cap who would then boo me as they passed. Stupid Notre Dame shorts, why did I wear them?

"Hey, Irish!"

I kept walking.

"Irish…Ammo…you got a second?"

Huh? I stopped and saw a middle-aged lady with curly brown hair and sunglasses. She was holding a camera.

"I won't keep you long, I promise," she said between pants. "I just want to thank you."

I didn't catch her name but caught her story loud and clear: "My dad went to Notre Dame…and he took me to all the Notre Dame games…and he…he died last year from cancer. I'm running this race for him…and I…I am so ready to give up. But then I saw you…and your Irish shorts…and your leg. I feel like he's up there telling me to not give up. It's like a sign, you know, Pop telling me to not give up."

She laughed. I laughed. We hugged and she took a picture of us and then one of the back of my shorts.

She then shot away before I could give her a business card or exchange contact info, I think because tears were streaming down her cheeks. Still, her dash away seemed more resolute and determined so I resumed mine.

Every few feet I would feel a hand on my back or shoulder, followed by someone running past me with a thumbs up and a smile. Some would yell out: *Way to go! You inspire me! Atta boy! God bless you, Team MADness!*

I would point to them with my drumstick, wink, thank them, and get back to feeling like I was about to die.

Keep pushing. I can't go further. Just keep pushing.

"Oh yeah! Way to go, A-Mo!"

Wait, someone said my name right. How'd they know my nickname?

I stopped and turned around. It was my friends, Jim Ponder and his daughter Kelly!

"Keep walking, keep walking!" They hugged me but exhorted me to not stop my journey. Jogging alongside me, they asked how I was feeling.

"Tired…very tired…but glad to see you guys."

"Alex, my man," Jim said, "you just keep walking. Don't worry about time or other people or anything but you. It's just you and God out here."

Kelly agreed and talked about how they had each done races individually but never as a tandem. I truly appreciated this father-daughter duo because they helped get my first book published, booked my speaking engagements, and more than anything were just great friends.

They were also very competitive and had set specific time goals. Not wanting to be the one that delayed those, I urged them to run ahead. With a fist bump from Jim and a hug from Kelly, they sped away. To see the people that helped me achieve the dream of publishing *Swinging for the Fences* was just awesome. I felt a jolt of energy.

That's how it continued for the next two miles. I would see other exhorters—cheerleaders, drink distributors, musicians—and their cheers would lift me for a good ten minutes. One cheer squad was sitting with their football-jersey wearing classmates and stood up to give me an ovation and offer high-fives and fist bumps. Many of those kids looked flat-out incredulous and I overheard one boy say, "Man, I'm never going to complain again."

Then my feet would start feeling like they were dragging through wet cement. All I could hear was other feet pounding gravel and my heavy breathing.

I did look up and smile, though. The skies had suddenly turned gray, a swarm of clouds quickly descending over the bayside. The marine layer arrived quicker than normal and by 2:00 p.m. it blanketed the city. It felt distinctly cooler, breezier, and fresher. My faith compelled me to thank God for this personal gift He had provided.

As people passed by me they also noticed my "SD" cap and would either yell out *Go Padres!* or *I'm a Red Sox fan but you guys are having a wicked awesome year!*

"Thanks!" I shouted back, "I work for the team!"

If they looked surprised or asked a question about beautiful Petco Park, I would stop and pull out a business card. This was great, marathon-ing and marketing all in one!

Every few yards, more questions came in, so more business cards came out.

My legs were still feeling heavy but I was too close to the goal now. One mile remained and the only option was to just keep my legs moving and see where I stood time-wise at the end.

With one final turn around Fiesta Island's circular slope, I knew I was one mile of straight pavement from the finish line.

"All right, Alex, no stopping now!"

It was a girl's voice I recognized and coming towards me?

It was a neon-green jersey. It was several neon-green jerseys–it was my MADness teammates! How sweet, they came back to walk the final lap with me!

"We came to get you," said Karen, "because in the distance we recognized your limp, even across the bay. And then we recognized you digging into your shirt pocket for business cards. That's it, no more cards…focus!"

She was right and I was just glad to see Karen, Alison, Colleen, and Colleen's boyfriend, Mike Adams. In tow with them was another co-worker, Trina Falvey, who snapped some action shots and three friends—Juli Long, Raquel Rodriguez, and Emily Nakayima—who had been volunteering since 4:30 a.m. but stuck around to root me on. I was allowed to give those four friends a quick hug and then they walked with us as Madden, Glabe, McEniry, and Adams formed a wall around me.

Of course, this meant people saw Team MADness walking as one and they cheered us like we were their favorite soccer team strolling into a stadium. *I love you, Team MADness! You guys rock!*

After four miles of walking in what seemed like near-desolation, I now saw and heard a swelling crowd. People traditionally gathered near the finish line to cheer for friends and strangers, lining both sides of a corridor, separated only by a chain-link fence. Having already finished their leg, my teammates couldn't go through the finish line so they told me they'd go around and meet me on the other side of it.

A man with a t-shirt that read *Team In Training Hawaii* came from behind me and just started taking all kinds of pictures. I could see a huge finish line banner erected by

Competitor Group and hear that near that banner they had a DJ and two announcers.

"Aw, yeaaaah, here comes another participant…give it up folks for…Team MADness!"

The crowd cheered and I could see my teammates near the final tape. Colleen held up a camera and I could tell the way she was holding it that she was filming. The DJ was mixing various beats and songs and just as I approached the finish line, I recognized "Sexy Back" by Justin Timberlake.

I stopped, danced, stopped again, took an imaginary swing, shimmied, and pointed to the heavens. The crowd came unglued. The announcers exploded in laughter. Karen and Alison shook their heads. I literally danced across the finish line.

"Oh my gosh! Oh my gosh!" Alison was looking at her watch. "A-Mo, you projected you'd be done in two hours and forty-five minutes, right?"

I nodded and caught my breath.

"You finished in two hours and *fifteen* minutes!"

Everyone whooped and I was stunned. "But wait," I interrupted, "I know we didn't get picked up…and there are people behind me so…did we make it under seven hours?"

Karen smiled and said, "Your favorite number is seven, right?"

She held up a digital runner's watch. It read: 6:53. That wasn't the time of day for it was just late afternoon. That was our composite team time. Six hours and fifty-three minutes. Or, seven under seven.

We did it. I bent over in exhaustion. Oh my freaking gosh, we did it!

THE FINISH LINE

After taking a boatload of group photos, chugging bottles of water, and finding out via Juli Long's cell phone that the Padres had rallied from behind to win that day in Philadelphia, my teammates and I went straight to Old Town.

This rustic part of the city, populated by bazaars, museums, and Mexican restaurants, was identified months ago as our post-celebration spot. Katie Leisz joined us at an outdoor restaurant called La Piñada and the margaritas and exultations flowed freely.

Alison was freaking out about a ladybug climbing her shoe, Karen was admonishing me for stopping along my route to talk to people, and Colleen was laughing at it all. When I previously wondered why I was putting myself through this race, the answer was right before me: this feeling of personal accomplishment and team camaraderie.

That's why you push to become a champion. You go through sacrifice, and self-torture, and doubt, and even physical pain so that you may grow. Be it in sports, business, arts, or education, you get comfortable being uncomfortable. You stretch and you grow. You teach yourself to keep pushing; do not quit; dig deeper; acknowledge the adversity; but keep moving forward. You do it for that one day you reach the top and it is exhilarating.

About ten days later I had a speaking engagement. This was a graduation speech in a gymnasium for middle school students in an inner-city institution named King-Chavez Academy. I soaked in the noise from the pulsating drum line and the heavy symbolism present; here I was in a school named after two of my heroes, Dr. Martin Luther King Jr. and Cesar Chavez, on a basketball court while 120 miles northward my favorite NBA team, the Los Angeles Lakers, were suiting up to play the Boston Celtics in a winner-take-all Game 7 of the Finals.

Clearly the connection of the civil rights leaders held far more importance than any sports analogy, but I mentioned both entities in my speech and I mentioned the Rock 'n' Roll Marathon. Believe in the sanctity of your journey, I told them, because along the way you may have people doubting you and you may doubt yourself. But if you have faith, and great teammates and leaders among you, and a goal set in mind, you can achieve anything. You can achieve *anything*!

The students cheered and clapped and as their ceremony concluded, the gym reverberated with celebration as they completed one academic level and eagerly anticipated the next. That night the Lakers completed a comeback from a three-games-to-two deficit in a nail-biting victory over the Celtics. I had noticed many friends taking shots at the team recently, and I certainly understood that they were a much-loved *and* hated organization, but I was compelled to write on my Facebook page: "It takes talent and even ego to win some games. But it takes heart and teamwork to become a champion. Final: Lakers 4–Haters 3."

Now I know my buddy Nick, who despises all things Los Angeles, will dislike that comparison but I felt a relation to the Lakers championship. Any sports season is a marathon and Phil Jackson, my all-time favorite basketball coach, assembled a unit that differed in talent level, experience, and personalities. He got them to buy in to the principles of sacrifice, teamwork, and simply playing for each other. In my mind that was sheer MADness.

Sunday, October 3, 2010.

The marathon had passed a few months prior and my teammates and I were focused on another race—the chase for the National League West pennant. It had been an intense season of baseball, culminating in a race down to the wire between our Padres and the San Francisco Giants.

Before the season and even into the season, all the analysts and experts projected we'd be out of it by July but here we were, on the last day of the season, only one game out.

Alas, we lost that game in the Bay Area 3-0 and the division title went to the Giants. It was two teams, fighting the odds, and going nose to nose, which meant euphoria for the winner and dejection for the second place club.

We were the second place club and it hurt. Our season was over.

At beautiful Petco Park we had invited our fans to come watch that game on the video board on a sunny and crisp early-autumn afternoon and they filled the outfield grass. As the game ended and the Giants celebrated, most fans filed out quietly.

As nightfall descended I went across the street to eat at Lolita's, site of so many fun Team MADness lunches, and then returned to the office to grab my work bag.

"You know what? This is crap. I know people are sad and disappointed but these players deserve to be told thank you and then goodbye."

I recognized both the voice and tone behind it. It was Karen Madden, still limping slightly and now hovering over my desk. Her arms were crossed.

"What," I sighed, "do you have in mind?"

She pointed out that I had a large network of people on my Facebook and Twitter accounts and within my cell phone directory. In fact, if ten people on each told ten people they knew, it would be immediate and exponential communication. The objective: get San Diegans down to Petco Park by 8:00 p.m. to greet the team buses and thank the players for a great season.

This idea was organic and intriguing but also late and sudden—it was already nearing seven o'clock. Really, it was madness.

Which is why we did it.

After getting internal approval from security and operations, we posted and texted messages urging people to come out. Colleagues like Alison and Andrea Smith did the same and news organizations caught wind of it. People made signs thanking the lads and streams of fans and camera men simultaneously arrived, forcing us to bring out metallic barriers for safety.

At 8:17 p.m. two large chartered buses pulled up and Padres players came out, with looks of weariness and surprise. As they and their wives walked into the indoor player parking lot, many stopped to shake hands with fans and take pictures. Flashes illuminated the night and cheers filled the air.

It was an end and a beginning, as all life events are.

The Giants went on to capture the World Series championship. Players like Adrian Gonzalez, Scott and

Jerry Hairston, and Tony Gwynn Jr.—his father having been diagnosed with cancer of the salivary glands while the elder Gwynn's "Mr. Padre" statue stood beyond centerfield as always—said goodbye for the last time as Padres. Closer Heath Bell, the colorful personality who recorded forty-seven saves, eventually signed with the Miami Marlins. The business of baseball can be crazy that way. The man standing next to him as they hugged fans, Bud Black, was soon named National League Manager of the Year.

Against a backdrop of skyline tinged in red, purple, and pink, as sunset clashed with starry nightfall, the off-season had begun. I counted about 200 fans there, not huge but also not bad for two hours' notice.

It was beyond disappointing to not make the playoffs. I didn't sleep well for the first week, lamenting what could have been.

But I was not any less proud of the guys or less grateful for the nine-plus months we had just experienced. As an organization we went from projected also-ran to stout contender, enjoying a thrill ride for the ages. Within that three of my best friends took a lesson from the team we worked and rooted for, and utilized togetherness and determination to beat the odds. We completed our very first marathon.

Sometimes the only acceptable goal is to bust through the finish line. Other times you have to appreciate the entire process, the entire race, and take the lessons you are given. Even in disappointment there can be victory.

I fist-bumped Karen and Alison.

Beating the odds? Proving people wrong? Reaching new heights and making the most of God-given opportunities?

Now *that's* MADness!

EPILOGUE

The 2010 San Diego Rock 'n' Roll Marathon was one of the greatest experiences of my life because it was one of the hardest. It required strict discipline, intestinal fortitude, and great determination. Competing on a relay team is hard; competing as a triple prosthetics-wearer is grueling.

But I learned so much about myself and about what can be achieved with the assistance and participation of others.

I often say that persons with disabilities need two things: opportunity and assistance.

We need to have the same opportunities that our able-bodied counterparts are given. This bodes true in education, business, and society in general. Athletics is no exception.

There is also no shame in admitting we need assistance, and the level of help needed varies from person to person and sometimes varies in each situation. My teammates were there for me and provided lifelong lessons in friendship, bringing out the best in others, and what it means to collectively achieve a goal.

But as noted in the final chapter, every end is a new beginning. Before two years had passed, each one of my MADness teammates had moved on to different futures.

Alison Glabe moved to Washington, D.C., to work for the Multiple Sclerosis Society. It was her first move outside of California and a major leap of faith—she loves it.

Colleen McEniry now works for Teamwork Athletic, a sports apparel company in San Diego. A year after our relay team she completed an entire marathon in Las Vegas.

Karen Madden became Karen Kawachi after marrying Ken in a ceremony in Japan, where his family resides. Early in the Padres season of 2012, she accepted a position with the Semper Fi Fund, which raises funds for marine and navy combat personnel who are wounded.

She still lives in San Diego and, in 2011, Competitor Group International reduced the relay teams from four persons to two and the relay course to that of a half-marathon (13.1 miles). Karen and I again donned our Team MADness jerseys and completed the course as a team.

After that initial race in 2010, each member of Team MADness completed at least one other endurance competition.

One of my biggest supporters each time I've done a subsequent relay team or 5K was my older sister, Elizabeth. In 2002, she had migrated from Colombia to Atlanta, where she got married and had two sons. Frequently she would tell me in 2010 that she wanted me to visit to show my race participation medals to her boys and husband.

After my second race in 2011, she told me the same thing. A few months later, I was headed to Atlanta. But not under happy conditions.

Elizabeth was diagnosed with colon cancer. It was stunning to hear, but my family knew she had a fighter's spirit and would battle it every step of the way.

For eight months she battled, as the Georgia peach trees gave way to autumn leaves, and then frost, and then lush greenery again. Finally, in the spring of 2012, as another baseball season had commenced, she took a turn for the worse. A number of family members, myself included, came from California, Florida, and South America to see her.

We were crestfallen to see her now skeletal body enduring daily amounts of medicine and agonizing pain. Cancer is treacherous to its victims and exhausting on the patient's families.

But we left after a week in Georgia feeling slightly encouraged. Elizabeth was in the hospital but still alive and still fighting.

Mama and I returned to San Diego, where the night air was as heavy as our hearts. It was the third weekend of April, and we flew back on a Friday. The next night I was being given a "Lead On" Award—bestowed to those who strive to educate others about living with a disability while displaying community leadership—by the wonderful local organization Access to Independence. In my brief acceptance remarks, said amid swirling emotions of pride and melancholy, I dedicated the award to Elizabeth.

The whirlwind continued as I got about four hours sleep that night (similar to race day) and woke up at 4 a.m. I was heading to the mountainous region of Idyllwild to deliver the closing speech to 350 high school juniors at the Rotary youth leadership camp. Not feeling particularly motivated, I resisted the temptation to cancel. Because, as I told the students, "We are blessed to be out of our beds, and moving and kicking, and my sister would give anything to do that right now."

I had flown into Atlanta unsure if Elizabeth would survive the week. I left there seven days later buoyed by the fact she was still alive.

The next few weeks were like riding an emotional roller-coaster. Telephone calls yielded the news that her energy had increased then lowered; her pain subsided then returned; her stamina had risen then plummeted. I prayed that God would somehow release her from this misery.

Weeks passed. Summer was beckoning, and Elizabeth was not getting any better. Suddenly, on June 6, two days before my thirty-eighth birthday, the news reached us that she had passed. Elizabeth was moving on to be with the Lord.

Our family felt anguished. Tears flowed, and, with grateful hearts, we accepted condolences from friends far and wide.

However, I also felt a sense of peace. Certainly my heart was grieving. But I thought back to the mid-April journey to Atlanta, where seeing Elizabeth's gaunt face indicated to me she wouldn't last past that week. The doctors and nurses noted, though, that having family there seemed to bolster her resolve. It motivated her. It gave her more reason to fight through the pain.

Seven is my favorite number, and Elizabeth had lived seven more weeks. We regarded it as a gift from God. She pushed and pushed until finally her body succumbed to the cancer. To me, though, it was a release. She was now released from pain and into the tranquility of heaven.

Sometimes you don't know where or when the finish line stands. But God does. And He gets us there. And then, onto another race.

PHOTOS

My first book, *Swinging for the Fences,* allowed me to make many new friends. I deeply appreciated their support.

With New York City Marathon champion and Olympic medalist Meb Keflezighi, a friend since junior high school.

Team MADness was fired up to race together!

Surrounded by teammates determined
to get me to The Finish Line.

We did it! Karen "K-Mad" Madden; Alex "A-Mo" Montoya;
Colleen "CoCo" McEniry; and Alison "AG" Glabe.